Living Room Revolution

Cecile Andrews gets to the heart of what we really need in America — a restoration of conversation about what matters in our lives. In this book, she shows how we can do it effectively using examples from folk schools to living room dialogues. I'm particularly taken by her ideas about the Pursuit of Happiness and how we can use "happiness circles" to analyze and improve well-being. Both thought-provoking and extremely practical, Cecile Andrews has a lively style, peppered with a ready wit, that makes her writing readable, brisk, and fun! I've been a fan of her work for years, and this book is no exception. It can help improve your quality of life!

> —John de Graaf, co-author of *Affluenza* and
> *What's the Economy For, Anyway?*

Don't be deceived by Cecile Andrew's niceness and reasonable tone. *The Living Room Revolution* is real revolution, showing how to communicate and why it's important for social change. Unlike most revolutions, though, this is one in which everyone wins. Cecile's approach has made a big difference in the Transition groups I've been in. We come away from group conversations energized rather than frustrated, and eager to do more.

> —Bart Anderson, Co-editor of the websites Energy Bulletin and
> Resilience.org and Co-founder of Transition Palo Alto

If the past several decades have taught us anything, it's that lavish wealth, invincible technology and unlimited information don't make us very happy. As Cecile Andrews shows in *Living Room Revolution*, happiness is centered on close friends, strong communities and convivial connections. This book is a handy, enjoyable primer on how to enrich our lives at the same time as making a better world.

> —Jay Walljasper, author of *All That We Share:*
> *A Field Guide to the Commons* and *The Great Neighborhood Book*

What a pleasure to read this book, I simply devoured it! Cecile Andrews has brought us a manifesto for cultural transformation through the renewal of our own satisfaction. She breaks it down for us; by using the tools we already have at hand, that we were born to use, we can help ourselves and each other reclaim and reinvigorate our communities. With her wealth of live experience in numerous movements, and insightful, broad focus, Ms. Andrews joyfully invites us to discover a robust and real personal expansion with each other as we remake our society. Great work, I am so inspired, thank you Cecile!

—Mark Lakeman, Co-Founder, The City Repair Project

The future starts with a conversation. How they're conducted, their purpose, and how we engage in them determines what kind of future we'll create. Do we have lopsided, purposeless conversations? Or do we have real dialog about matters of substance where everyone is heard? There's no way society will change positively unless the answer to the latter is yes. *Living Room Revolution* shows the way.

—Neal Gorenflo, publisher of *Shareable*

Reading Cecile Andrews' books has often been compared to having a conversation with her. *Living Room Revolution* is literally about conversation — how it can fill the yearning for a better world and spark the transformation we all long for. Small groups. Study circles. Stop 'n chats. House parties. Movie nights. Online sharing. Bring people together, and you never know what kind of fuse you'll ignite for change. *Living Room Revolution* gives you that excitement of waking up on a sunny morning, saying to yourself, Yes! There really is hope — and today I'm going to make a difference!

—Wanda Urbanska, co-author of *Less is More* and author of *The Heart of Simple Living*

Modest in style, Cecile Andrews has taken on the most fundamental question that plagues movements for social and cultural transformation: why are they not sustained? Her answer is both simple and profound — only that which sustains the spirit will endure. Experiential rather than theoretical, she brings a lifetime of activism to her reflection, and offers a central pivot for those who would build movements, great and small: convivial conversation — genuine, life affirming engagement that allows us to find joy in the other fellow. To have such conversation is a way of going through life, and Andrews has lessons to teach for those who would master the art.

—Jerome M. Segal, author of *Graceful Simplicity: The Philosophy and Politics of the Alternative American Dream*

Living Room Revolution

A HANDBOOK FOR
Conversation, Community and the Common Good

CECILE ANDREWS

new society
PUBLISHERS

Cover design by Diane McIntosh.
Background image: © iStock (tulcarion); Sofa image: © iStock (jallfree);
Doodle illustrations: © iStock (katyakatya)

Printed in Canada. First printing March 2013.

Paperback ISBN: 978-0-86571-733-6
eISBN: 978-1-55092-532-6

Inquiries regarding requests to reprint all or part of *Living Room
Revolution* should be addressed to New Society Publishers at the
address below.

To order directly from the publishers, please call toll-free (North America)
1-800-567-6772, or order online at www.newsociety.com

Any other inquiries can be directed by mail to:

New Society Publishers
P.O. Box 189, Gabriola Island, BC V0R 1X0, Canada
(250) 247-9737

New Society Publishers' mission is to publish books that contribute in fundamental ways to building an ecologically sustainable and just society, and
to do so with the least possible impact on the environment, in a manner that
models this vision. We are committed to doing this not just through education, but through action. The interior pages of our bound books are printed
on Forest Stewardship Council®-registered acid-free paper that is **100%
post-consumer recycled** (100% old growth forest-free), processed chlorine
free, and printed with vegetable-based, low-VOC inks, with covers produced
using FSC®-registered stock. New Society also works to reduce its carbon
footprint, and purchases carbon offsets based on an annual audit to ensure a
carbon neutral footprint. For further information, or to browse our full list
of books and purchase securely, visit our website at: www.newsociety.com

Library and Archives Canada Cataloguing in Publication

Andrews, Cecile

    Living room revolution : a handbook for conversation, community and
the common good / Cecile Andrews.

Includes index.
ISBN 978-0-86571-733-6

    1. Conversation--Social aspects--Handbooks, manuals, etc. 2. Social
interaction--Handbooks, manuals, etc. 3. Social change--Handbooks,
manuals, etc. 4. Community life--Handbooks, manuals, etc. 5.
Happiness--Handbooks, manuals, etc. 6. Joy--Handbooks, manuals, etc. I.
Title.

P95.45.A54 2013   302.34'6   C2012-906881-0

Contents

Dedication

To my little dog, Maggie, 1996-2012.

Acknowledgments

Acknowledgments always begin by saying there are count-
less numbers of people to thank. This is particularly true
this time. I want to thank all of the people over the years who
have gathered in my living room for good conversation. They
all inspired me.

In particular, though, I want to thank my neighbors in
Seattle with our Phinney Neighborhood Center and our
Sustainable Greenwood Phinney neighborhood group. I think
what we're doing can inspire the whole country. The same goes
for Transition Palo Alto and our Community, Calling and
Conversation circle. Bart Anderson, one of the members, kept
insisting on the importance of my message about conversation
and community! And Barbara Weinstein used the phrase *living room democracy* as we were talking one day — making me
think, "Yes! a *Living Room Revolution*"!

Of course I want to thank New Society Publishers for its
commitment to supporting ideas for a transformed society. And
I want to thank them for always providing the atmosphere of a
good living room conversation — warm, cordial, and personal!

And boring though it is, I want to thank my husband, Paul.
I have time to write and be involved in community education
because he does almost everything that keeps our lives running. (He brings it on himself, of course — he's just better at all
the practical things than I am, so he gets to do them!)

But this last acknowledgment is hard. For sixteen years there was a constant presence in all my living room conversations — my little dog, Maggie. After greeting everyone she curled up at my feet while we talked. She died this year. Who knows how her presence affected all of us as we talked? Maybe when we connect to our own species, we can better connect to all of the species. Or is it the other way — when we connect with other species we'll connect better with our own. Either way, it's how we'll save the planet.

Preface

*Many things indicate that we are going through a
transitional period, when it seems that something is on
the way out and something else is painfully being born.
It is as if something were crumbling, decaying
and exhausting itself, while something else,
still indistinct, were arising from the rubble.*

– Vaclav Havel (In memoriam)

At the heart of this book is the notion of convivial, caring
conversation. To my mind, it's what will save the world.
It's what brings us together. It's what will help us go from a
culture of "You're on your own," to one of "We're all in this
together."

Conversation seems like such a basic thing, but most people rate our national conversation skills as very low. What's
happened? For one thing, many of us are concerned about our
counterfeit connection — connection to screens instead of to
people.

At the same time, if there's ever been a role for the Internet,
it's now. Things are happening so fast out there that any book,
frozen in time as it is, is out of date almost immediately.
I'm writing the final draft of this in the spring of 2012, and
I oscillate between despair and joy, reflecting Vaclav Havel's
observation — despair at the possible fate of our planet and

our people, joy over the changes and new ideas emerging around the world.

Because things are moving so fast, some ideas I barely introduce and encourage you to Google to find out more. But that's OK, because my goal isn't to fill you with facts and information. I'd like to see this book as an opening to a conversation. I'd like to get you talking to the people around you, and *I'd* like to hear from you as well.

In fact, I often think that my role is to revive the oral culture. Before print took over, talking together meant thinking together. Nothing was set in stone — in print. You could keep revising, and everyone had a role in creating knowledge.

When print came in, ideas were controlled by the elite — the people who could read and own and publish books — and ideas were frozen into place. The commoner no longer had the same role in creating and generating ideas.

But with the Internet, we commoners (people who believe in the commons!) have another chance. Elites have less and less control over ideas. We now have citizen journalists, citizen researchers, citizen philosophers.

And I think the Internet can spur a lot of face-to-face conversation. I know, I know — it cuts us off from each other as well. But it has a role to play and we need to build on it.

Some books may need to play a different role these days. Maybe they will be mainly an introduction to a larger conversation. I certainly hope that's the case here.

So I hope to hear from you. Better yet, bring a group of people together to talk about the ideas in this book and let me join in for a visit via Skype or Facetime. Just send me an email at cecile@cecileandrews.com and let's talk.

A book is certainly not the last word. And hopefully, no one will ever have the last word.

Chapter 1

Joy in the Other Fellow

*Democracy, in the American tradition, has been defined
by a simple morality: We Americans care about our
fellow citizens, we act on that care and build trust, and
we do our best not just for ourselves, our families, and our
friends and neighbors, but for our country, for each other,
for people we have never seen and never will see.*
— George Lakoff and Glenn Smith, in "Why Democracy
Is Public: The American Dream Beats the Nightmare"

*Yes, we pay a lot of taxes, but we don't mind
because it allows us to care for each other.*
— unidentified Swedish citizen

A few years ago, something happened to me that I haven't
been able to forget. It was no big deal, yet it has come to
seem emblematic of so many of our problems.

What happened was this: My husband and I were turning
left into the parking lot of a grocery store. As we turned, we got
stuck blocking traffic, and we were faced with a dilemma. On
the one hand, there was a parking place close by, but we could
see another driver heading for it. On the other hand, we could
see another slot she could take a few spaces away. Since we
were blocking traffic, we slipped into the closer place, forcing
the woman to take the other spot.

We got out of the car and were walking toward the entrance when the other driver started yelling at us. "You really had a lot of nerve taking my spot!"

My husband, wiser than I, just ignored her. But I tried to explain and apologize. "We're really sorry," I said, "but we were blocking traffic and could see there was another spot you could take." (I did not add, "as evidenced by the fact that you just parked there.")

"That was just plain rude," she yelled back.

I continued to try to explain, but then we arrived at the entrance and took our grocery carts. Grabbing hers she screamed, "Get out of my way, bitch!" and rammed into my cart.

Well, there we were. The doors slid open and all the lines behind the cashiers stopped in their tracks. They could hear every word, and they were all stunned.

The manager rushed over, asking if I was OK. I, of course, burst into tears.

Now, this incident wasn't really anything big. But the more I've thought about it, the more I've come to see how it signifies much that's wrong with our culture — in particular, our cut-throat competition, our sense that we should take whatever we want, regardless. The woman thought that the parking space was hers. She was there first and she had a right to it. She couldn't stand that she lost out. She should have won and she felt justified in being violent.

This is our culture. "Every man for himself!" "Get yours before anyone else does." We compete over everything: getting a parking spot, getting the best grades, getting the most money, having the most power. We want to win, often at any cost.

And what does that lead to? Last one standing! We're destroying ourselves and our planet. I don't need to elaborate on the problems of our no-holds-barred approach to life: climate change, environmental devastation, poverty, unhappiness, and wars.

We know we must change. We must understand that we need each other — we must learn to collaborate and care for each other. We need a new culture in which we realize that "we're all in this together." (I hesitated to use this phrase because it can sound like a cliché. I've chosen, instead, to see it as a rallying cry.)

Ultimately, that's what this book is about. *Changing our culture so that we care about each other and the planet.* Doing something about our selfishness and greed. Changing our cutthroat competitiveness by building more cooperation and collaboration. Creating a culture in which people care about the common good.

Hope

Part of the problem is that, at some level, we don't think there's hope. We've pretty much concluded that human beings are a failed species, that we're essentially selfish, and that there's nothing we can do about it. Certainly the things I've heard all my life make it difficult to feel hope — things like "survival of the fittest." Competing to win is what life is all about and always has been.

But in the past few years, a lot of scientists have been arguing that history shows that evolution favors cultures that trust and cooperate. Noted biologist E. O. Wilson, in his book *Social Conquest of Earth* (2012), says that evolution shows that groups that are cooperative are the groups that survive. Wilson bolsters his case by referring to Darwin's *Ascent of Man*, published 12 years after *The Origin of Species*, which argues that cooperation was the key to human evolution.

But wait — I thought Darwin talked about "survival of the fittest," which we have interpreted to mean that we can do anything, no matter the consequences, to get what we want. Actually, Darwin *didn't* use that phrase; apparently it was Herbert Spencer who coined it. Our early capitalists picked it up, with John D. Rockefeller referring to the conduct of business as "survival of the fittest." Rockefeller called it the law of nature and a law of God. Andrew Carnegie, in an 1889 essay "The Gospel of Wealth," saw survival of the fittest as best for the human race.

So, it's in our American blood.

But Darwin said that evolution favored cooperation because "selfish and contentious people will not cohere, and without coherence nothing can be effected."

This is surprising, isn't it? It gives us hope that human beings *can* be cooperative and collaborative. In fact, there is a lot of evidence that supports this.

History

The most dramatic evidence comes from history. Apparently, when faced with disasters we turn to each other. We take care of each other. We saw it in England during World War II, in the US during the Great Depression, even during earthquakes and snowstorms. In her book, *A Paradise Built in Hell: The Extraordinary Communities that Arise in Disaster* (2009), Rebecca Solnit tells the stories of disasters — from the 1906 earthquake in San Francisco to Hurricane Katrina and 9/11. Many of the stories come from people's own words, and in describing their experiences and emotions people used words like *euphoric* and *ecstatic* and *transformative*. What people felt in the disaster — more than fear and anxiety — was an astonishing caring and connection with others. She says that this capacity for community is an essential part of our nature kept buried by conventional society, and that disaster can allow something to emerge that has been there all the time.

As Solnit quotes one young woman in the San Francisco earthquake saying,

> Most of us since then have run the whole gamut of human emotions from glad to sad and back again, but underneath it all a new note is struck, a quiet bubbling joy is felt. It is that note that makes all our loss worth the while. It is the note of a millennial

good fellowship.... In all the grand exodus ... everybody was your friend and you in turn everybody's friend. The individual, the isolated self was dead. The social self was regnant. Never even when the four walls of one's own room in a new city shall close around us again shall we sense the old lonesomeness shutting us off from our neighbors. Never again shall we feel singled out by fate for the hardships and ill luck that's going. And that is the sweetness and the gladness of the earthquake and the fire. Not of bravery, nor of strength, nor of a new city, but of a new inclusiveness ... the joy in the other fellow.

Institutional Change

That's it! How do we get people to feel "joy in the other fellow"? How can we turn to the cultivation of caring as one of the most important things we must do? A lot of recent research suggests that the institutions and policies we create can influence people to be more collaborative, cooperative, and caring.

For instance, Harvard law professor Yochai Benkler, in his book *The Penguin and the Leviathan: How Cooperation Triumphs over Self-Interest* (2011), even has some percentages. According to him, about 30 percent of the population behave as if they really are selfish. "Fully half of all people systematically, significantly, and predictably behave cooperatively." Most of us, he says, could go either way, depending on our surroundings. Some people are kind only when others are kind, and selfish when others are selfish. Some are committed "cooperators or altruists."

Benkler concludes that there has been practically no society in which the majority of people have been consistently selfish. Given the right conditions, people will cooperate and collaborate — of their own free will — to serve the collective good. We need to figure out the "levers" or "triggers" that will evoke cooperation and collaboration.

Essentially, it depends on the cultural norms and institutions. Do they encourage selfishness or caring? In the US we design our systems with the assumption that people are selfish, and that becomes a self-fulfilling prophecy. Our institutions, from businesses to schools, are controlled from the top, with the assumption that the main reason people act is to get rewarded, usually by money. But research shows that systems that are hierarchical, punitive, and incentive-based are not as effective.

What we need, according to Benkler, is systems that focus on *connecting people and creating a sense of common purpose and identity*. We must bring people together in ways that evoke empathy, solidarity, fairness, and trust. The more people get a chance to cooperate, the more they believe in it and the more they do it. They begin to see themselves as cooperative people, and they break the self-fulfilling prophecy of greed and selfishness.

Benkler gives us real-life situations that illustrate this. For instance, apparently people are less likely to give blood when they are paid for it. Feeling that you are contributing is a greater reward than money. (In fact, there's long been evidence that shows that giving people extrinsic rewards for intrinsically motivated behavior can discourage the behavior.)

Benkler also tells the story of a Toyota plant that took over a failing GM car plant and turned it around because they went from an assembly line with every move scripted to a system where people worked in cooperative, democratic small groups.

So there are strong arguments that if you want change, you change the institutions.

And there's more support for this approach. Harvard professor of psychology Steven Pinker, in his book *The Better Angels of Our Nature: Why Violence Has Declined* (2011), argues that we live in the least violent time in human history. According to his research, we are increasingly less likely to die in war or in personal violence. In particular, he shows how things have changed in our life time. For instance, it is no longer acceptable to lynch a Black man; it's no longer acceptable for a husband to beat his wife; it's no longer acceptable, for most of us, to spank our kids.

But why? He argues that it has to do with certain changes: First, a state monopoly on force made a difference. (By and large, we don't seek our own revenge, but use our courts.) In addition, the spread of commerce reduced wars. (Why kill off people who might buy your product?) Further, he thinks the invention of printing affected us because it spread progressive ideas, and novels like *Uncle Tom's Cabin* and *Oliver Twist* evoked empathy about the plight of others. (I've often thought my social conscience was born in reading *Little Women*.) Finally, we've learned through the ages to use *reason*, and therefore we can think through the consequences of our behaviors and see that shooting the other person would not really benefit us in the long run.

I am particularly interested in the last two because these are two strategies we all can easily build on: evoking empathy and using reason. This is what I'll explore in this book: how to create opportunities for empathy and reason through conversation, community, sharing, education, and more. But with a difference — we don't have to wait for the experts, the elite, the most competitive. It's us. We can create new ways of carrying out these age-old traditions. Ways that are more participatory, inclusive, egalitarian, and enjoyable. We, the People! Not in our own backyards, but in our own living rooms.

So, there we have it — a biologist, a law professor, and a psychology professor arguing that our true nature is not based on competitive greed. But economists, the most traditional of the bunch, are weighing in as well, arguing that *a selfish, winner-take-all approach to life doesn't work as well as concern for the common good.*

Massachusetts Institute of Technology (MIT) economist Daron Acemoglu and Harvard political scientist James Robinson, in their book *Why Nations Fail* (2012), argue that throughout history nations *that were not economically and politically inclusive failed.* If a small group of people at the top controls everything, both economically and politically, no one else has a reason for even trying. For instance, if the small farmer works harder and the increased wealth all goes to his boss, why should he do more work? If the citizen speaks up and is ignored, why should he keep trying? Countries that become too unequal will fail.

Authors Richard Wilkinson and Kate Pickett, in their book *The Spirit Level: Why Greater Equality Makes Societies Stronger* (2009), develop this idea further. They show that in unequal societies there's more violence, mental illness, incarceration, obesity, unwed pregnancy — and, ultimately, shorter life expectancy. Even the rich person in the US doesn't live as long as the poorer person in Denmark. This is because inequality undermines social cohesion. In unequal societies people are less trusting and caring, more competitive and fearful. People become more isolated, stressed, and depressed — and unhappiness is catching.

So ultimately we must work for more wealth equality. But that's a long-term project, so in the meantime, we need to work at creating institutions that give people a taste of equality. We need to give people experiences of cooperation and collaboration. It's something that we can all do. All of us can join in to create community in our lives. In community people learn to cooperate, collaborate, and care. We need to remember the words the young woman wrote about the San Francisco earthquake. We need to work for a "new inclusiveness ... the joy in the other fellow."

A New Vision

So maybe things are more hopeful than most of us have come to believe. Yes, we believe that people are essentially selfish — that if you don't look out for yourself, nobody else will, that it's "every man for himself." This is certainly the philosophy that dominates our lives. But accepting this view is certain doom. It's a philosophy that benefits the wealthy and the powerful.

Why? Because it diminishes the hope that people have — the belief that we can come together and work with each other for change. If you believe that selfishness and greed are inevitable, why try to change things?

But there is hope because there is much evidence to show that human beings are not basically selfish and greedy. If we reward people only for competing, they will compete. But if we give them a chance to cooperate, they will cooperate. When they see that things get better when they collaborate, they'll collaborate more.

When they see that people care about each other, they'll change their belief system and become more hopeful. When people are hopeful, they're more likely to act for the common good. So a positive circle of change begins.

We need to change the way we think and at the same time change the institutions that make us think that way. We must create experiences that evoke empathy, solidarity, fairness, and trust, as Benkler suggests — experiences that also give us the opportunity to reflect and reason in a new, participatory way.

Let's explore how we can do this.

Chapter 2

Real Happiness

*Because if your main goal is making money, you have time
for nothing else and become a "cripple in a cave."*
— Virginia Woolf

In the previous chapter we explored what history, psychology,
and sociology are telling us about human nature. But there's
one area of new research I saved: happiness. New books have
flooded the market. Why? Because we've reached the point
where we're beginning to realize that our ideas about happiness haven't worked. They're wrong! We've been operating with
a faulty map of reality.

For instance, we've believed, very deeply, that if we're rich
we'll be happy. This sums up our approach to life. But most of
the problems we face, such as poverty, wars, corruption, and
even a lot of poor health, are a result of putting profit ahead of
the well-being of people and the planet. We commit so many
crimes for money. And it doesn't even make us happy. Research
shows clearly that, after a certain point, more money does not
make you happy.

Our "gospel of wealth" has failed us. If we let this belief
continue to guide us through life, we're lost. But think about
how deep this belief is — we can read a story about people
winning the lottery and that they're ecstatic for the first week.
But by the end of the first year, they're not only less happy,

often their lives have fallen apart. But when we read such a story we think, "*I* would have been an exception. I know *I* would be happy if I were rich. *I* could handle it !" Even though the belief is inaccurate, it is very deep.

Earlier I referred to one of the best books on this subject: *The Spirit Level: Why Greater Equality Makes Societies Stronger,* by a pair of English academics. (It doesn't have anything to do with spirituality — in Britain, "spirit level" is the term for the level that carpenters use to see if things are even.) The book is about the effects of inequality that have been measured by years of research. The authors gathered all the research and came up with some surprises. What is particularly surprising is that it's not just the poor who suffer from inequality — we're all victims. As Nobel economist Joseph Stiglitz says, when inequality gets too great, the society becomes so unpleasant that even the rich won't like it.

Here are some of the shocking findings:

Physical health: People in more equal countries live longer, and fewer children die in infancy. It's not just the poor. Rich people in the US don't live as long as the average person in a more equal place such as Denmark.

Mental health: World Health Organization surveys find that in more equal countries five to ten percent of adults have suffered from mental health issues, while in the US, more than 25 percent have.

Drug abuse: People in more equal societies are less likely to use illegal drugs.

Prison: No surprise here. More prisoners in unequal countries. For instance, the US imprisons people at 14 times the rate of Japan, a fairly equal country.

Obesity: In the US, three quarters of the population are overweight and almost a third are considered obese. This, of course, affects physical health, with obesity leading to diabetes, heart problems, and a range of disabilities.

Education: When countries are more equal, students do better at school. In particular, the US has more high school dropouts and lower levels of test performance in math and science.

Violence: Homicide rates are higher in unequal societies, even among children. In the US a child is killed by a gun every three hours. US teenagers have the highest rate of violent death in the western world.

Trust and community life: This is really the key to all of the above. In unequal societies, there is less trust and less caring because everyone feels they're competing for limited resources. They worry that if they don't get their share, someone else will grab it. They don't care who they trample on to get what they want.

In particular, inequality fuels status competition. Everyone is fighting to be considered "somebody." We often respond by trying to put others down. It's very stressful to feel that others think they're superior to you. And in a culture of status competition, no one wins. There is always someone above you. If indeed some make it to the very top, no one likes them anyway. The higher up you go, the more people feel envy and greed — not healthy emotions.

So, when people are unequal, their emotions are negative. Everyone feels more stress — isolation, loneliness, anger, anxiety, envy, and greed.

Ultimately, we must do something about wealth inequality. Without addressing this, there will be no chance of creating a caring, collaborative culture concerned about the common good. In fact, as we saw earlier, according to books like *Why Nations Fail*, an oligarchy eventually plunges a country to its death.

Happiness Research

In the previous chapter we discovered that being selfish and competitive is not our essential nature. From the happiness research we can see that being selfish and competitive doesn't even make us happy. Let's look at the findings.

Unfortunately, when we talk about happiness, we need to start by being on the defensive. Why? Because for some, even *talking* about happiness seems shallow. There are so many problems — climate change, poverty, injustice, war. How can we even think about happiness? But there's evidence that happy people are more likely to vote, more likely to be better parents, more likely to care about the environment, more likely to be cooperative and caring. And happy people are healthier. (Maybe showing how much we would save on health care costs would convince people.) Happiness, then, is good for people and the planet, so it behooves us to work for happiness.

Happiness Decline

Unfortunately, happiness in America has been declining for the past 40 or so years. A recent Gallup poll comparing 151 nations placed the US 69th on sadness, 74th on anger, 89th on anxiety, 145th on stress. Only a few countries are worse than we are on stress — and they are probably in the middle of a famine or a civil war.

Ironically, Americans still claim they're happy. When asked about how happy they were, respondents ranked the US all the way up at the 11th spot. It's as though Americans want to see themselves as happy, even when they're not. What does this mean?

It means we're confused about happiness. When we equate happiness with the conventional idea of success — having money and status — we tend to rate ourselves as happy, even though we may be *feeling* angry and anxious. It's because we don't want to see ourselves as losers. Of course we're happy. Look how well we're doing. And thus, we lie to ourselves. But when we're honest about how we actually *feel*, we're not doing so well.

So let's take a look at the research and see what happiness consists of. I've discovered in my reading of the research that there seem to be four main factors in happiness, all very related: connection, calling, celebration, and control. (Some people get carried away with the Cs and start listing things like chocolate, chuckles, or Camembert cheese.)

So here they are. To be happy, people need these four Cs:

Connection: People need social connections with others, including family, friends, and a civic life.

Calling: People need work — whether paid or not — that brings them meaning and purpose.

Celebration: People need to experience enjoyment and delight in their daily activities.

Control: This one is more complex. Basically, having control means having the ability and opportunity to meet your basic needs of safety and survival and self-respect — being able to make goals and accomplish them. It means having the ability to influence the decisions that affect us in our community and work-place. It means sharing our ideas and opinions and feeling we are being listened to. It means acting on our values. Obviously, it means living in a democracy.

On the personal level, people need to keep their lives from slipping out of control by managing things like debt, clutter, or time deprivation. They need to clarify their goals, discover their values, and learn how to act on them. They need to be able to find work, afford education, and have medical care available to them. Many of these are related to societal forces, something we have little control over. This leads us to talk about "cultural" happiness — or Gross National Happiness — which we'll explore in a little while.

Let's look at the four factors in more depth.

Connection

The chief predictor of health and happiness is social ties. Study after study confirms this. Social ties correlate with health, happiness, and longevity. People with stronger social ties get sick less, depressed less, and enjoy their lives more.

And, not surprising — as happiness has declined, so have social connections. People are more alone and isolated than ever before. We have fewer friends: a quarter of people have no one to talk to about matters of substance, and another quarter have only one person. Some research has found that social isolation is as bad for you as smoking. In fact, some of the evidence is quite striking. In his landmark book, *Bowling Alone* (2001), Robert Putnam, a Harvard sociologist, says that if you aren't in a group now, and you join a group, you cut in half your chance of dying within the next year. (Now, you may not have had a big chance of dying, but still ....)

Research says that depression has increased tenfold in the past generation, and at same time community has gone down. We have fewer picnics, potlucks, or family dinners than we used to.

What's interesting, though, is that people say they're depressed, but they seem unable to recognize that they're lonely. Jacqueline Olds and Richard Schwartz's book *The Lonely American* (2009) points out that doctors give patients pills instead of asking them why they're depressed. Actually, neither the doctors nor the patients may recognize the connection between depression and loneliness. It's just not the way Americans look at life. One psychiatrist said that he regrets all the time he spent with his patients talking about their early years and the damage from their parents. He says he would have been more helpful if he had worked with them to find new friends. Understanding our need for other people is missing from our worldview, but the new research is very clear on this.

Calling

For most of us, this is probably easier to understand than social ties. Most of us realize that to be happy, we need to have something that gets us excited, that we feel enthusiastic about, that brings us a sense of meaning — something we feel is really us. It's like the universe calling out to us, saying, "Do this!" You can't even force yourself to like it — you either do or you don't. It's like falling in love. Having a passion is a basic source of life energy that spreads over into everything.

If people are pursuing their passions, they are less likely to pursue the false idols of profit, power, prestige, war, corruption — substitutes for the real thing.

Having a passion makes you kinder and less envious. You don't notice if people have more status and wealth because you feel fulfilled.

Getting involved in a group or project and finding your kindred spirits builds social ties.

For some of us it's the arts; for some it's social activism; for some it's physical activity. We're drawn to it because it gives us energy and makes us feel more alive. It becomes our calling when we feel we are also making a difference.

In fact, some refer to this involvement as the "activist cure." When people are lonely or depressed and find a way to make a difference, either by volunteering or getting involved in social change, it helps alleviate their own difficulties. One of the best examples is the story of the founder of Mothers Against Drunk Driving whose daughter was killed by a drunk driver. She was unable to overcome her despair until she founded this powerful organization. (Not only did she make a difference, she formed connections with others who had suffered what she had.)

To help us understand this puzzle, we can turn to a book called *Why Good Things Happen to Good People* (2007). Author Stephen Post writes about the growing body of research that shows that kindness, caring, and generosity are good for health, happiness, and longevity. As he puts it in his final chapter, "Give and be happier. Give and be healthier. Give and live longer." Over and over the studies show that "good" behavior helps not only the recipient but the giver. People who are kind and caring score higher on all sorts of measures of happiness, health, longevity, self-esteem, and creativity.

So how do you discover your calling? By exposing yourself to different experiences and new people. Does something pique your interest? Then find out more. Seek out new experiences — go to meetings, take classes, sign up to volunteer or work on a campaign. Hang around enthusiastic people and see what you can learn. Enthusiasm is catching.

Whenever I do something, I look at my energy level. Does it give me energy or sap me of energy? As Henry David Thoreau said, "Discipline yourself to yield only to love; suffer yourself to be attracted."

Of course our schools and our culture are so regimented that it's easy to miss out on finding your calling. Whenever we do something because we're rewarded for it — or punished if we don't — we're not engaged in our calling. Whenever we do something to impress others, to build up our status, it's not our calling. And that brings up our earlier comments by Benkler, author of *The Penguin and the Leviathan*. Most of our institutions, including schools and the workplace, are set up on the basis of reward or punishment, not intrinsic satisfaction. No wonder we pursue wealth and status instead of our calling.

Social connections are important in finding your calling. We often learn about ourselves through other people. For instance, *my* particular calling seems to be bringing people together in small groups. As one friend said when she saw me starting, yet again, another small group, "You must have been a sheep dog in a former life!" I remember thinking, "Yes! How nice to know your true nature."

I remember understanding my path to happiness at an early age. I've always had a rule: Do more things you enjoy; get out of things you don't enjoy; and try to enjoy whatever you do.

Certainly I've always gotten out of unpleasant things. I discovered this tendency when I realized that whenever my friends didn't want to do something, they called me. They called me because they realized I would give them permission to say no! They would call me and say, "I've been invited to be on an important board, and I know it would help my career, but I really don't want to do it." I'd say, "Tell them no!" Or maybe it was a promotion that meant they'd have to travel and leave their young children. "Tell them no!"

I remember thinking, "This is weird —   do I have a

reputation as a slacker?" Why were they calling me? I realized that I *did* get out of a lot of things. In grad school I'd talked my way out of statistics. I got out of dull meetings while I was a college administrator.

So I realized I had a particular talent of escaping unpleasant things. But where did it come from?

I realized it was something that happened when I was very young. Our family was living in Germany when I was five and started kindergarten — which I didn't like. I went home and said I didn't want to go anymore. My father said, "If she doesn't want to go, she doesn't have to." (He started me on my career as a slacker.)

When I was eight, my father died in a plane crash. Later in life I would remember that as a turning point — I learned to never waste my time on things that didn't matter. Because who knows how much time we have left?

Then when I was 16, I saw Thoreau's words:

> I went to the woods because I wished to live deliberately, to front only the essential facts of life, and see if I could not learn what it had to teach, and not, when I came to die, discover that I had not lived. I did not wish to live what was not life, living is so dear; I wanted to live deep and suck out all the marrow of life.

Our problem, I fear, is that our sense of life has been so diminished and trivialized that we never really feel what Thoreau expresses when he says "And not, when I came to die, discover that I had not lived."

We need to spend time on what's important and on the things we enjoy. And that brings us to the next C. We need the ability to celebrate.

Celebration

People who are reading this book are probably like me: we grew up really focused on being productive. If our teachers told us to do it, we did it. We learned to measure our time in terms of how much we had read, how much we had written. In terms of achievement.

This is a particularly American trait, thanks to our Puritan heritage. The Protestant work ethic derived from both religious sources and economic factors. First, our Calvinist religion maintained that our fate — heaven or hell — was preordained. But naturally, we wanted some clues about where we were going, so we began to believe that if we were successful in our work, God must be on our side. Thus, if you worked hard, it was a way of proving to yourself that you were going to heaven.

Second, not only were we dominated by religion, there was a lot of work to be done in those early colonial days! We needed some way to get people moving. Proving to yourself that you were going to heaven instead of hell was highly motivating. (Bertrand Russell said that this belief system was also the way that rich people got poor people to do the work for them. Sounds reasonable to me.)

That work ethic seems to have undergone some change, though: now people tend to focus more on things like wealth and productivity to prove that they are part of a new kind of anointed — people with high social status!

But still, we're not a culture that enjoys the moment. Mexico has been rated a happier country than the US in part because they don't have that Protestant work ethic. They tend to know how to enjoy themselves more.

Celebration involves savoring the moment, being curious, having enthusiasm, and appreciating the beautiful. Certainly, we all need to have enjoyment in our lives in order to feel happy — it's the *felt* experience of happiness. Of course, there are different kinds of enjoyment — it might be a moment of solitude as you stand gazing out on a lake; it might be a moment of joy as you listen to music; it might be a feeling of absorption as you read a novel. It could be reading or drawing a picture or playing a sport.

Or just sitting there. Central to celebration is the ability to reflect, to contemplate, to discern, to notice, to learn — something not really a part of American culture.

Celebration is related to what psychologist Mihaly Csíkszentmihályi calls *flow*. It's a deep absorption that brings you energy and joy. And of course, in our distracted society, it can be difficult to experience flow. We have too many emails, too many commercials, too many worries about money. So, the ability to celebrate is also related to control — in particular, control over your time.

But most of all, celebration is related to connecting with other people — coming together to laugh and talk and enjoy life together.

Control

The relationship of control and happiness is a little more complex, and maybe more subtle. *Control* is not an obvious need when thinking about happiness. In fact, it's more of a "negative" factor — it's that being *out of control* brings you unhappiness. For instance, if you're in debt, if you're very overweight, if you are overwhelmed by clutter, you feel out of control of your life and you're less happy.

Control at work is a huge issue, and we often speak of burnout — feeling stressed, tired, crabby, and sick. Control factors that contribute to *burnout* are lack of job security, failure of safety nets for the unemployed, the enormous gap between pay for CEOs and for others, and lack of wage growth. Certainly sounds familiar.

This shows another dimension of happiness. Some things *are* out of our control. It's not a personal issue but a societal issue. There are real reasons to feel overwhelmed — our economy has produced long work hours and job insecurity. We need government policies to control things. Further, you have a feeling of control when you work to change things.

The problem is that in this culture we're encouraged to see things in terms of personal failings — if you were only smarter, more attractive, or more savvy, you wouldn't be having problems. What's wrong with you anyway? Try a little harder. Take a few pills and you'll feel better. But often the answer lies in changing the society around you.

Control even extends to the larger culture: if you are involved in a democracy and have a say in the decisions that affect you, you tend to feel more in control and are happier. And this introduces a key element in all we're talking about — the need for policies to create this new culture.

Inequality

In particular, as I discussed earlier, inequality creates unhappiness. Although this subject is increasingly receiving attention, Richard Sennett and Jonathan Cobb told us about it in their book *The Hidden Injuries of Class* (1993). Sennett and Cobb agree with Thorstein Veblen — rich people don't acquire wealth just to consume goods they like; they want to display their wealth to indicate their social superiority.

Feelings of social worth motivate us all. Sennett and Cobb interviewed working class men and found that being at the bottom of the occupational scale robbed them of their dignity, even when they earned enough to live on. They coped with this lack of dignity by claiming social superiority from their families — they were in control; they must be obeyed. Most blamed themselves for failure in the workplace, but there was one place they could make it up — in their families.

Sennett's work has been magnified by Wilkinson and Pickett in *The Spirit Level*. They show that everyone is affected by this desire for dignity — a feeling of self worth that's related to control. We all want to be respected and admired, but it's very difficult in an unequal society, because there's always someone above you. You're always in danger of slipping down a rung. As we saw, wealth inequality is the biggest predictor of things like violence, drug addiction, mental illness, incarceration, and longevity because wealth inequality undermines the feelings of control one has over one's life.

Inequality is relevant to all facets of happiness. We feel more bitterness, envy, and resentment when we're around people with more power and wealth than we have. We find it harder to find careers that give us a sense of calling. (Too many people are forced to work for giant corporations that have few morals about what they do to people or the planet.) Inequality means that people work longer hours, giving them little chance to celebrate. Feelings of worry over money or health care or unemployment make it difficult to celebrate life. And of course control: in the past we felt optimistic because we felt that if we worked hard, we could get ahead. Now that feeling is lost.

So ultimately, we can't just look at the issue of personal happiness, but at the policy implications of happiness. This is what the new movement for Gross National Happiness advocates.

Gross National Happiness

The Gross National Happiness (GNH) movement is working to help us develop "happiness" measurements for new policies — similar to the concept of environmental impact measures. In this movement, governments test their policies not just in economic terms of GDP (money flowing through the system) but in terms of the happiness they will bring the community. They focus on the areas of psychological well-being, physical health, time balance, work experience, education, arts and culture, environment, government, as well as community and material well-being. It's very important, with the exploding interest in the topic of happiness, that we work to help people see that we must go beyond individual change and create institutional and policy changes as well. John de Graaf, author of *Affluenza (2005)* and *What's the Economy For, Anyway: Why It's Time to Stop Chasing Growth and Start Pursuing Happiness* (2011), is one of the leaders of this new movement. He works with the Happiness Initiative to help us understand that we must work for institutional as well as personal change.

Obviously, addressing wealth inequality would solve many of our problems, but in the meantime, we also need to work on the problems of fair taxation, climate change, unemployment, and funding of things like education, parks, and health care. Fortunately, getting involved in working for the common good is one of the most satisfying human behaviors, and it brings you community, calling, celebration, and control.

One of our founding fathers expressed it well: "A good government implies two things," wrote James Madison in 1788. The first is "fidelity to the object of government, which is the happiness of the people." The second is "a knowledge of the means by which that object can be best attained."

Chapter 3

Convivial Community and Social Change

*[F]unctioning democratic communities of mutual support
... that's what's lacking in our country; that's why we don't
have a functioning democracy — a community of real
participation. That's really important.*

— Noam Chomsky, May 4, 2012

*When the Stranger says: "What is the meaning of this city?
Do you huddle together because you love one another?"
What will you answer? "We all dwell together to make
money from each other"? or "This is a community"?*

— T.S. Eliot

Convivial Community

A few days ago, the weather was perfect. Sunny and around 72 degrees. We took Maggie, our little bichon frise, out for a walk, but not a usual walk. She's old and walks very slowly, and sometimes decides not to walk at all. So we take her in a stroller.

Now, if you want to guarantee that you'll experience the heart of convivial community, just try walking your dog in a stroller. Everyone we passed stopped us to chat, smile, and laugh about our dog, about the weather, about anything at all.

I realized that a feeling of happiness was welling up. For a little while we were all united in our joy of the beautiful afternoon and the convivial community.

Convivial community — what a wonderful ring to that phrase. Certainly, all the research indicates one thing: to survive, we must come together and create a caring, collaborative culture. And it appears, as we learned from recent research, that it's possible. Human beings aren't as selfish and greedy as much of our behavior and belief system would indicate. We can look at our behavior throughout human history and see that we have survived because we collaborate and cooperate and care.

But with climate change, we're at the brink. We can't wait for evolution to run its course and produce a more cooperative human being some day in the distant future. We must throw ourselves into an all-out attempt to learn cooperation and caring now.

How do we create change through community?

When I do workshops, I ask the participants to recall times in their lives when they experienced community, and to reflect on how it felt. As I listen to their responses, the word that always comes to my mind is *conviviality* — the quality of being companionable, congenial, agreeable, and amiable.

I've always loved the word *convivial*. Maybe because it's related to the Latin word viver, to live. It's an energy that involves people and bathes them with good will. It's a concept that points the way in our search for a way to nurture caring, collaboration, and concern for the common good. We need to create convivial community.

Convivial is a word that is related to *empathy*. People like Berkeley's George Lakoff have repeatedly said that if we want to bring about a more caring culture we must create empathy — a connection with others, an understanding of others.

To bring about change, we must give people *experiences* that evoke empathy. The best way to do that? Create convivial community — build a culture in which people *experience* what the San Francisco survivors felt — "joy in the other fellow."

Confused Thinking

Now, you'd think people would understand how important community is and take every opportunity to connect with others. But we know that people *don't* understand. Too many of us still think, at some very deep level, that fame, wealth, and power will make us happy. I grew up thinking that *studying* was always the best use of my time — studying so I could get good grades. Or reading so that I could write something. Being with my friends was something I did (at heart I'm a hedonist), but ultimately I didn't believe that it was really important.

But as we've seen — and the happiness literature is clear — it is social ties that make you happy.

Since people don't understand this, how do we educate them? We have to lure them in, evoke in them a desire to live in a new way by giving them the experience of community. Let them see how important it is by experiencing it. Then, as people's lives change and they become happier, they'll be more empathic and caring, more committed to community, and we'll create a new culture.

Importance of Community

We need to realize that there are lots of reasons why community is important. Community meets the basic happiness needs of connection with others. You feel happier; you feel safer; you feel you belong. But it also meets the needs of the common good as well — it's through community that you can get people interested and concerned about the greater good. Robert Putnam was very clear that the culture in which people talk over the back fence is the culture in which people vote. We can no longer separate individual and cultural happiness. Those people talking over the fence are happier because they're connecting, and democracy is benefitting because more people are voting and involved. People who are engaged in their community are not only happier, they are better citizens.

For social change, then, creating convivial community is where we start — not as a separate thing, but in anything we do. Anything that brings people together not only benefits them individually, but benefits society as a whole. For instance, a friend of mind has on his email the tag line, "If you want to create a new culture, throw a better party." I think this is what we have to do.

Social Change

When we're working for social change, we often forget the importance of community. We focus on goals. We're here to win an election, to save the old-growth forest, to get people to drive less. But the change either doesn't happen or it doesn't stick because the change isn't linked to community. We drop out because the meetings are tedious and unpleasant. People find excuses for not coming.

But it doesn't have to be that way. *No matter what you do, make sure people get to know each other and talk with each other in a congenial way.* For instance, always start your meetings with conversation and tea and treats, taking time to move around the room and greet people. Start your meetings with a "check in." Periodically have small-group discussions in your meetings so that everyone gets to talk and make closer contact with others. Hang around at the end for convivial conversation. Periodically have potlucks. Make the meetings enjoyable. Establish guidelines that keep the meetings amiable and interesting — not more acrimonious or dull meetings to sit through.

For example, a few years ago our neighborhood took on a corporation that wanted to build a huge parking lot in a very inappropriate place (as if there is an appropriate place). We came together and worked and had rallies and contacted city hall and passed out literature and had meetings, meetings, meetings. And we won! It was people coming together that made the difference. We enjoyed ourselves thoroughly because we did it through convivial community. Yes, we got our business done at meetings, but at the same time, we laughed and talked together. We worked together in a way that was supportive, enjoyable, and egalitarian. We became very fond of each other and experienced "joy in the other fellow."

We also need to create convivial community in social protests! When we try to change society, often our first impulse is to denounce and attack with anger. But this doesn't attract people — it just makes them angrier and more likely to withdraw. Instead, we're discovering what does motivate people in a positive direction: something that gives them a sense of delight and enlivenment — having fun. Take, for instance, flash mobs.

Not long ago I participated in my first flash mob, protesting the Afghanistan war. We were told to report to a downtown shopping mall at ten minutes before noon. We were supposed to mingle with the shoppers and then take our places. It was an open court with three floors of balconies, and we gathered around the edges so that we could look down over the whole mall.

First of all, it was kind of funny. We were supposed to blend in with the shoppers so that no one would notice what was happening. But it's a pretty upscale mall, and we all dressed as we usually do — for comfort and not for style. We all looked pretty much like we had just come in from gardening. So you could pick us out.

And some did. We talked with the shoppers, telling them we were working for peace. They seemed interested, particularly because those of us involved are pretty nice people. Then, right at 12 noon, the leaders gave the signal and we all began singing. We sang three songs. Unfortunately, we seemed to know the words to only one song — "Down by the River Side" ("Ain't Gonna Study War No More"). We did a pretty good job on that. The other two were a little weak.

And then, within ten minutes, we were out of there. We left just as the police arrived. (Demonstrations on private property aren't allowed.) But the police couldn't have picked us out, anyway (despite our clothes). *Everyone* was smiling and laughing. It was so much fun. We enjoyed ourselves and it was communicated to the shoppers. If this was someone's first experience of a political protest, it must have won them over to our side for sure.

And of course it was posted on YouTube for all the world to see.

Certainly it brought the joys of happiness — *community* (we were taking a risk together), *calling* (we were taking an action that brought us a sense of meaning), *celebration* (we were laughing and singing together), *control* (whenever you act on your values, particularly as a citizen, you feel greater control).

This is the sort of thing we have to keep doing if we want to create a new culture. We need to come together in activities that evoke empathy and enjoyment. No more dull speeches at rallies. No more ranting and raving.

If we do have marches, they need to be like San Francisco marches with giant puppets and lots of color and lots of singing. In earlier marches my husband carried Maggie in a backpack with a sign that said, "Bichons against Bush." (In later marches her signs read "Bichons Bark for Barack.")

The important thing to realize is how fulfilling it is to gather with people who share your ideals, to join in solidarity with others to make a difference and experience community.

Occupy Movement

And it seems that those in the Occupy movement realize this.

As I write I have no idea what the future of Occupy is. But why did it capture people's imaginations so strongly? I think because in the gatherings people felt the presence of connected, convivial community; they experienced people coming together and caring about each other and about the fate of the planet. Seeing people camping out, forming a lending library, setting up a first aid station, and on and on, moved us. Many people I know visited New York and were affected by what they saw. It brought back the vision of Martin Luther King, who talked about the *beloved community*, and of course for many of us the civil rights marches transformed our lives.

In an article posted on Common Dreams on April 30th, 2012, Sarah Van Gelder, editor of YES! Magazine, talks about Occupy May Day plans of fairs and fiestas and music and art and food and "flash occupations." Van Gelder concludes, "This broad range of topics and tactics may bewilder mainstream pundits, but it reflects a transformation in activism as profound as anything that's happened in social change over the past decades."

Noam Chomsky, in an article for GritTV, on May 4, 2012, talked about two different strands in the Occupy movement — both of them important:

> One is policy oriented: what policy goals [do we want]. Regulate the banks, get money out of elections; raise the minimum wage, environmental issues. They're all very important and the Occupy movement made a difference. It shifted not only the discourse but to some extent, action on these issues.
>
> The other part is just creating communities — something extremely important in a country like this, which is very atomized. People don't talk to each other. You're alone with your television set or Internet. But you can't have a functioning democracy without what sociologists call "secondary organizations," places where people can get together, plan, talk and develop ideas. You don't do it alone. The Occupy movement did create spontaneous communities that taught people something: you can be in a supportive community of mutual aid and cooperation and develop your own health system and library and have open space for democratic discussion and participation. Communities like that are really important.

It's clear that an essential way to stop the violence and the despair in our culture is to engage in activities that bring us empathy and conviviality. The vision of convivial community will attract more and more people.

We can't have demonstrations every day, but there *are* things going on every day that we can be involved in, in particular, the movement for sustainability through building local community.

Localization

I've been talking about organizing for protest and political change. Convivial community is particularly important in these areas because it's so easy for people to fall into angry and aggressive tactics. But there's another movement growing that's involved in working for social change — localization. Eating local, buying local, living local. A perfect example of conviviality. It's creating the caring community right in your own backyard, right in your own living room. It's crucial for bringing about changes for sustainability and addressing climate change.

Convivial neighborhood communities are growing all over. Take a look at the book *Superbia* (2003) by Dan Chiras and Dave Wann. They describe neighborhoods having community dinners, community newsletters, neighborhood clubs for investment or gardening, babysitting co-ops, car pools, work/share programs, and tool sharing. Neighbors plant trees together, retrofit homes together, and one neighborhood even bought a local house and made it into a community house. Now it's a place where they have group dinners, share office space, and rent out space to local small businesses.

All this at a neighborhood level. And of course you can go further and explore co-housing where people buy homes in a complex with a community house and open spaces for gatherings. The co-housing movement continues to grow, particularly for baby boomers who are looking for new ways to live in community as they age. There's also a "village" movement for elders that gives them the services they need and allows them to stay in their homes.

Anything you do to bring people together makes a difference. You're helping create a culture where people feel they belong. One thing you could do right away: plan an emergency preparedness gathering. As climate change increases, we face more and more weather disasters. Most cities have programs to help you prepare. But after you do the first one with a city representative, follow up with something different.

That's what I did not long ago. We'd already had someone from the city speak to us a few months earlier. Yes, she was very informative, but essentially, we all just sat there, listened, and went home. In our next meeting we all talked, got very excited about our plans, enjoyed each other, and went home planning to get together again soon on a social basis.

I shouldn't have been surprised at how exciting it was. I've been involved with educating adults for many years, and we are not passive learners. You learn better when you're involved. But, you're saying, What did you do without a speaker?

Well, first we reviewed what we're supposed to do in an earthquake — I simply asked everyone to contribute what they knew and we covered everything. (I had prepared myself with information ahead of time.) Then we talked about how to actually *do* it. We realized as we talked that the way we act in an earthquake involves more than following a script; it involves judgment — being able to make a snap decision based on the information you have. You can't prepare by memorizing a bunch of rules; you have to prepare by brainstorming — thinking and talking together ahead of time.

For instance, one woman talked about how, in a recent stay in a motel, she noticed a big picture above her bed. She took it down because she knew this was one of the biggest risks — being hit by a falling object. (Her teenage daughters laughed at her, but I'm sure they learned a good lesson.) Another person told how, when he goes to Costco, he tries to imagine what he would do in a quake. There are stacks of things there that could fall on you, but holding up the stacks are sturdy steel frames. He's diving into one of those. Others had more ideas.

We talked about lots of things: where to store our water, what kinds of foods we were getting, what to keep in our car. We passed on new ideas we've learned: for instance, if you're in bed, you're not supposed to get under your bed — as we had been taught in earlier classes — you're supposed to stay in your bed and pull the covers over your head. And no door jambs any more either!

The point was that we shared what we knew with each other. We talked together and created a sense of conviviality. The most helpful thing we discussed was what things we need to do *together*. Most of the official training assigns roles to people. But who knows who will be home (or uninjured) when something happens. We agreed that we would gather on the triangle of grass in our street and figure out things together.

And we laughed a lot. When we went home that night we talked of meeting monthly at a local coffee house just to get together. The big lessons we learned are that we don't have to only rely on experts, that we all know a lot more than we think, and that we need to come together to share what we know. And we need to enjoy ourselves together by creating convivial community. All the ingredients that trigger happiness and collaborative behavior were there: telling our personal stories gave us connection; working together for the good of the community gave us a sense of meaning; laughter brought a sense of celebration; and certainly emergency planning is focused on taking control of your life.

So find a way to bring people together. For anything and everything. Have meetings on emergency preparedness; or share garden ideas; or explore ways to slow down the traffic. We invite our neighbors over for comedy movie nights where we come together and laugh. One of my favorite events is *news* night. In our weekly news night we come prepared to tell about one news event that happened that week that we're excited about. (This year we're going to feature clips from Jon Stewart and Stephen Colbert.) We all need a chance to spout off among friends. Further, you're more likely to keep informed if you know you have someone to talk with. Certainly one of our goals in a democracy is the informed citizen.

Probably my favorite event, though, is our "unbook club." You just get together and talk about what you've been reading. You don't worry about everyone reading the same book — making some of us feel guilty because we haven't read the assigned book. (My husband often cheats, though, and talks about a book he's *planning* on reading. No one remembers to check up on him at the next meeting.)

In building local community, you'll get a lot of good projects done, yes. But more important, you'll build a new culture that is cooperative, collaborative, and caring.

Public Places

Earlier I talked about how I ask people to tell me their experiences of community. I start with an example of my own to get them going: my experience in graduate student housing called Escondido Village, on the edge of the Stanford campus. It's built in a series of circles — apartments built around green spaces with a playground in the middle where the kids could play. Our sliding glass doors opened out onto patios and picnic tables at the edge of the green. I realize that I loved it because there were always people there to talk with. There was always someone there with their kids. You didn't have to make a date; you could just wander out.

Lately, people have been realizing the importance of public spaces, places for people to gather and just hang out. As the mayor of Bogota, Colombia, says, "The least a democratic society should do is to offer people wonderful public spaces. Public spaces are not a frivolity. They are just as important as hospitals and schools. They create a sense of belonging. This creates a different type of society — a society where people of all income levels meet in public space is a more integrated, socially healthier one."

One of my favorite examples of this is "parklets" in San Francisco. Taking up only two parking spaces, the designers are able to create seating for up to twenty people by ingeniously placing small tables and benches next to each other. Whenever I've sat down at one of the spaces I've always had wonderful conversations with a stranger sitting next to me. You can't avoid it because your knees are almost touching!

And this is what it's all about. Do everything you can to give people a chance to come together, to interact with each other. There's a story about one of Steve Jobs's projects: he insisted that the center of the building be a large atrium and that everything connect to it. All the offices opened on to it; the conference rooms had windows that looked out on it. Even the bathrooms connected to it. Why? So people would interact. So people would run into each other and start talking. Steve Jobs knew that this is where the creativity and new ideas came from — connecting people.

We need to do this on a large scale as well. We can work to create opportunities in cities for people to mingle and talk — plazas and parks and outdoor cafés. When you talk to strangers, you learn to care for people you have never met. Caring for the stranger is an underlying factor in creating a culture that cares for the common good.

For instance, years ago Portland, Oregon, remodeled its downtown, putting in a huge public square with the big department stores opening onto it. I've often wondered — was this one of the reasons Portland became such a sustainable and community-oriented city? (Visit the website of Portland City Repair and see how they're drawing people together.) Whatever the reason, sustainability and community are related. Even though the people sitting in the plaza enjoying their morning coffee don't necessarily realize they're participating in democracy, they are. Find out more from Project for Public Spaces.

So whenever you can, create places where people will run into each other. Support efforts to narrow the streets and widen the sidewalks so people can hang out. But most of all, act on this yourself. Be an example. Spread democracy and happiness! Have lots of "stop and chats." Walk through your neighborhoods and stop and talk with people. We got this idea from Larry David, the creator of *Seinfeld* and his own TV show, *Curb Your Enthusiasm.* He hates "stop and chats." He's such a curmudgeonly guy that when he sees someone on the street he goes to the other side so he won't have to interact.

The book *Consequential Strangers* (2009), by Melinda Blau and Karen Fingerman, shows the importance of this seemingly insignificant behavior. Just chatting with people as you go through your day makes you happier and healthier.

And think of the social statements you can make. I often see my husband engaged in what I've come to call "grocery-line activism." He has these cute hemp shorts that he wears, and people always compliment him. So he tells them about hemp and how good that is for the environment. One day I saw him in a line with everyone talking. The cashier was saying how important hemp is; the bag person was blaming the large corporations for fighting against hemp. I thought, "He's got a little revolution going right there!"

"Grocery-line activism" led to the idea of "elevator ambush" — always carry a newspaper with you so you can refer to some headline; when the elevator door closes, you make some comment on a story about the Tea Party, and then when the door opens, you're out of there before any conflict can start.

Or how about "cell phone subversion." You know how loudly people talk on their cell phones on the bus? Well, you don't even need to make an actual call. Just talk into your phone about how awful it is that we're spending so much money on war, and how that needs to change.

Or finally, how about "café conversion" where you talk about the importance of income equality in a slightly loud voice so the people at the next table can hear you. You never know what might happen. I've had people join a conversation.

We can make a difference each day as we engage in convivial conversations.

Transition Movement

Localization is one of those movements that is growing so fast that it's not much use describing it in detail. Just Google it and you'll see that there's lots happening. In fact, a similar movement is also growing by leaps and bounds and is helped tremendously by the Internet. It's called the Transition movement (originally Transition Towns, but now it's in cities all over the world).

Started in England, it's spreading around the world with Transition Initiatives. Like Occupy, it's decentralized, egalitarian, participatory — the central ingredients in community. The name refers to the need to make a *transition* to a society in which we use less and less oil — responding to climate change and the fact that we're running out of oil.

That's at the heart of it, but it's not *what* we dwell on that is important. We focus on creating a new caring community. Transition participants recognize that joyful community is the central thing that can lure the affluent away from their consumerism — which, of course, is based on oil. So while Transition groups might have programs on energy reduction, they are just as likely to have a garden-share program, encouraging people to come together to create gardens and share their produce.

In particular, Transition has a "reskilling" program — reviving some of the skills people had before we started depending on machines. There might be a class on canning or sewing or gardening. There's certainly nothing that evokes laughter like teaching city slickers some basic survival skills. We just don't have a clue. Cooking together can be hilarious because some of us are really inept and the only possible response is laughter. I particularly like the idea of reskilling classes because it recognizes the fact that we can learn from our past. Too often we dismiss our past — calling people Luddites — and fail to learn valuable lessons. Perhaps if we learn to care about our ancestors, we'll also care about our descendants.

Ultimately all of Transition activities are about reskilling — rebuilding our abilities to come together, work together, care about each other.

And Transition is truly participatory. I remember some years ago having a program that included a panel put on by a similar neighborhood group. I asked them how they decided what programs to run. They said, "We don't make decisions." I loved it! If someone wanted to offer something, they put it on the calendar. If people came, great. If no one came, it didn't happen. This gives everyone a chance to be involved. There are no acrimonious arguments about what to offer. Everyone is much more relaxed and laid back than that.

That's the way we've run the Transition Initiatives in which I've been involved — in a participatory, decentralized, laid-back fashion (Transition Palo Alto, in particular). For instance, we get together to discuss the book *The Transition Companion* (2011), by founder Rob Hopkins and friends, but we're just as likely to discuss something that wasn't even in the chapter. (None of the oppressive tactics of so many literary book clubs — where people roll their eyes if you've said something off the topic!) Everything is related to everything anyway.

I literally have an opportunity to go to a Transition group almost every night. One night is the book club, another a study circle on sharing, another called "Transition Looks at Occupy," another called "Community, Calling, and Conversation."

That last one may be my favorite. (You may not be surprised to hear that it's one I started.) It's a group of supportive and informed friends we can explore our ideas with. It's like a support group for activists. You can talk about your particular passion and get ideas — with no pressure or judgment. And you know that people are on your side. Because we feel strongly about being supportive, the usual competition for who's smarter or more liberal is pretty much absent (even in Palo Alto).

A few nights ago we gathered to see the new film, *Transition 2.0*. About 12 of us sat around my living room enthralled. People from all over the world were having the same experiences we had been having. We had all become involved because of our concern about climate change and finding ways to get the society to use less oil. But we were tired of boring lectures and the attempts to make us feel guilty — tactics that weren't really changing our behavior that much. We had discovered in Transition a movement that understands that what changes behavior is community. The central theme of the film was inclusiveness — the idea that everyone has something to offer, the realization that you need support if you want to change, the understanding of how much fun it is to have real conversations about real things.

People in the film said things like "We talked into the night, and afterwards I was walking on clouds." A poor Black woman told how her street had changed as a result of a community garden; now she was proud of where she lived. "It's changed me," she said as tears rolled down her face. In a small town in India, people talked about how important it was to know your neighbors, how you felt safer and happier. One town had had a devastating earthquake and the local currency program helped them recover; people said they were drawn to Transition because it was more like a party than a protest march.

After the film, we did our usual: went around the circle responding with what we felt, what we thought — our heartfelt response. Everyone was moved and felt affirmed. We realized that a lot of groups fall apart because people can't get along. We realized that we had practiced "preventive care" by setting up convivial conversation guidelines from the first, guidelines that allowed us to overcome the usual jockeying for position (conversation guidelines that we'll soon discuss).

We all agreed that the important thing wasn't *what we had accomplished, but that we had changed.* We live more sustainably because we have been nurtured by the good will that flows from the group, experiencing "joy in the other fellow."

The film ends with this sentence: "If we want change, relying on the government will be too late; relying on individuals won't be enough; community is our only hope."

The Together Revolution

We're learning that we're *better together.* When we come together we make a difference and we're happier.

Community grows from whatever we do when it's done in a convivial manner — from potlucks to book groups. In fact one of the countries judged to be the happiest is Denmark, where 95 percent of the population is in some sort of group. Robert Putnam found that the more clubs and organizations that existed, the more responsive government was to its citizens.

There is some very exciting research that helps explain the power of community. Nicholas Christakis and James Fowler, in their book *Connected: The Surprising Power of Our Social Networks* (2009) show that we tend to *become similar to the people we're around.* The media focused on one of their studies and got lots of attention — research that found that if *your* friend loses weight, you are more likely to lose weight, and your friends will as well. People are affected by the people they're around. (So choose your friends carefully!)

Another book is called *Join the Club,* by Tina Rosenberg. If you want to change something, form a club that people want to join. She essentially describes how to use peer pressure for positive results. *Join the Club* shows that you can use people's tendency to conform for the betterment of society. You can use it in a positive way by forming clubs that are fun to join. She shows how people formed teen anti-smoking clubs in Florida and saw a dramatic decrease in teen smoking — something that's been almost unheard of in teen anti-smoking campaigns. This approach was used in India to make villages healthier, and even led to the fall of Slobodan Milosevic in Serbia. In all cases the groups, or clubs, that were formed were something cool to belong to. And in particular, they did things amazingly similar to our "flash mobs." The teenagers in Serbia would perform pranks and street theater — obviously forming a convivial community where there was much energy and exuberance.

Those of us involved in social change must use this strategy. We must form groups that are "seeded" with strong, exuberant individuals that others will emulate — maybe an enthusiastic gardener, or a person who feels strongly about political participation. The people in the group will become more like that person.

Equality

And finally, let me return to where we started this chapter — thinking about the experiences of community we've had. I frequently use my story about graduate student housing because we truly were "all in the same boat." We were poor students;

our apartments were all about the same size; and we all had to cope with families as well as graduate school. We were underdogs together. We were equals.

And in fact, as people in my workshops tell their stories, that's one of the things that always emerges. In community people are equals. As I said earlier, one of the biggest predictors of happiness and well-being seems to be equality. Usually we're experiencing the negative effects of inequality, but community allows us to understand what equality is like. (Once we know, we don't go back.) People feel the most comfortable with each other when they are equals. Inequality always puts up barriers because it causes resentment or fear or envy. And this is the genius of community — it's not community if it's not equal.

In equal societies, people understand that what hurts one person hurts everyone. It really is *all for one and one for all*. If one person has enough, everyone has enough. In unequal societies, everyone is pitted against everyone else for scarce resources. It's "every man for himself." Every day people feel the slights — however unconscious — of the people above them, and it's a wearing stress that doesn't go away, even though it comes to seem normal.

We've all felt this — the feeling that we don't count as much as the other person. I was once a visiting scholar at Stanford, and it was a very unpleasant experience. When I was a student, we were all pretty equal and we all truly felt that we were "all in it together." But as a visiting scholar from a community college (and my doctorate was only in education) I felt, acutely, my lowly status.

That was a strong lesson to me. As progressives, we're committed to equality, but if you live in this country, you feel the effects of inequality, because there is always someone above everyone. No one escapes. Being a part of a community mitigates that. Ultimately we have to work to change economic inequality, but that will be hard. In the meantime we must give people experiences of equality within community. Give them back their self-respect by treating them as equals.

Living Room Revolution

And we can do this, of course, with the Living Room Revolution. In her book *Alone Together: Why We Expect More from Technology and Less from Each Other* (2011), Sherry Turkle, a professor at MIT, talks about the negative effect of technology on conversation. In an article for *The New York Times* (April 21, 2012) called "The Flight from Conversation," she says this: "I am a partisan for conversation. To make room for it, I see some first, deliberate steps. At home, we can create sacred spaces: the kitchen, the dining room." Make your living room into a sacred space, a public space. This has happened a lot lately with MoveOn and the Coffee Party and other groups where people hold house parties in their living rooms. I've done this many times and felt no worry at all about having strangers come.

Random Conversation

Talk to everyone. Make the whole world your community. Have this be the centerpiece of everything you do. Find ways for people to talk with each other. If you have a meeting, make sure your planning committee greets people as they come in. If you have a film series, have people turn to each other at the beginning and introduce themselves. At the end of a lecture, have people gather in small groups of three or four just to chat for a few minutes about their reactions. Just having a discussion with the large group won't work — the same old people stand up and rant. Don't plan an event unless you plan a way to get people to interact. No one should leave an event without talking one on one with someone else.

When I think about how I originally got involved in activism, I realize it was because I felt there was more "life" in the people I met. I was drawn to them. I liked the way they treated each other. They looked like they were enjoying themselves. They were convivial.

I grew up in a suburb where people hardly talked to each other (except maybe to complain that a neighbor had left a garbage can out too long). I felt as though these were "corporate" people — all image and no substance. I felt I didn't get to know anyone who was really alive. But I discovered "alive" people in social change movements — civil rights, the women's movement. People involved in convivial community and social change are truly alive.

So the word *conviviality* — "with life"— is central to the way I live. The difference now is that I realize that *everything is activism.* It's not just participating in protests; it's the way I meet and greet people throughout the day — spreading conviviality.

There's a quote I've always loved: "We must learn to view the world through a social capital lens," said Lew Feldstein of the New Hampshire Charitable Foundation and co-chair of the Saguaro Seminar. "We need to look at front porches as crime fighting tools, treat picnics as public health efforts and see choral groups as occasions of democracy. We will become a better place when assessing social capital impact becomes a standard part of decision-making."

A Strategy for Us

We can spread social change conversation by conversation, smile by smile, laugh by laugh. And we just have to straighten up our living rooms a little so we can have people over. Not much to ask. (Actually, I try to have an informal, far-from-perfect look so that people always feel comfortable when they come to my living room. They think, "Well, if she can have people over, so can I.")

Environmentalist and author Bill McKibben says we won't have sustainability without community. Until we see other people as our main source of security, we'll keep turning to things — using up oil and other resources and polluting the planet. Until we can drop in on neighbors and hang out in the living room, we'll keep going to the mall for our evening's entertainment. Perhaps it's very simple — unless we learn to care for our own species, we won't be able to care for other species.

Chapter 4

The Sharing Revolution

The Beginning of a Sharing Movement

Not long ago I was invited to a clothing swap. I didn't really know the people, so I felt a little awkward going. But I did know one person there and she walked me through it. Essentially, I could take anything I wanted. I only took a few things because I'm really a committed minimalist, but — not surprising — the best thing about it was standing around and chatting with the other women. I realized that the new sharing revolution gives us lots of new ways to interact with others and build community.

For instance, I remember how my daughter's college, the alternative Evergreen State College in Washington State, always had a "free" box. You could take or leave what you wanted, and it was a great way to get to know people. If you saw someone walking across campus wearing your old shirt, you could go up to him and compliment him on the shirt, telling him how much better it looked on him than you. (Not a bad line, really.)

The sharing revolution is happening in all sorts of ways. My local neighborhood center has a tool bank and a mystery book exchange. We, ourselves, have done house exchanges with people in London, Berkeley, and Palo Alto. My neighborhood bought a chipper together, and we lend our truck to our neighbors.

It's funny how a movement can start and you don't even realize it.

The sharing movement is a big one, and it's getting bigger fast. The sharing movement is much like the Transition movement — it's participatory, enjoyable, and full of energy and new ideas. It's another way to lure people into creating a culture that cares for the common good.

Let me give you a little background.

Several years ago the Green Party in England faced a dilemma. People were buying washing machines for themselves and abandoning the laundromats. The party leaders knew that moving away from the collective to a private good was bad for the planet — more things being consumed, more resources being wasted. But they couldn't figure out what to do. Lecturing or scolding people didn't seem to work. (In fact, we now know that when people hear bad news about the environment, they quell their anxiety by going shopping.)

But a few years ago a man in San Francisco came up with a way to solve the dilemma of the laundromats. Jeffrey Zalles made his laundromat, called Brainwash, the place to be. There's a café, happy hours, live music, stand-up comedy nights, pinball machines, and of course free WiFi. He's built a sense of community where people come together and enjoy themselves. Instead of lecturing people, he's luring people by offering them the conviviality of social connections.

This story is in a great book called *What's Mine is Yours: The Rise of Collaborative Consumption* (2010) by Rachel Botsman and Roo Rogers. The book explores the new efforts that allow us to build social ties by *sharing* with each other — reducing consumption by giving people what they really need: connection with others.

Take the idea of *couch surfing*. When you're traveling, either domestically or abroad, you can go on the Web and find places to stay — free — in people's homes. The traveler saves money and gets to know the local community, and the host has the enjoyment of meeting someone from another culture. Good conversation flows and long-term friendships develop.

There are lots of free things like this. There's Freecycle, where you post online items you want or want to get rid of. On Craigslist you can find also find free stuff, as well as barters and house swaps. There are systems set up to help you carpool, rent out your car, or exchange books or clothes.

These free transactions are known as the *sharing economy*. Other transactions involve money and are referred to as *collaborative consumption* — an approach that gives people *access* to things, but since they don't need to own the items, it costs less. For instance, there's a "Netflix" sort of company that deals in children's toys. You just have a few toys, and when the child wants something new, you send one back and a new one arrives in its place!

This new movement helps us cut back on consumerism, reducing consumerism's negative effects on the environment and people's economic stability. The brilliant thing is that it works. Haranguing people about consumerism doesn't work. Shaming them doesn't work. Fear doesn't work. Conviviality and community work!

More and more, people are beginning to understand that social connection is the biggest predictor of health, happiness, and longevity. The more friends you have, the better your life. So any practice that brings people together in a congenial fashion — like sharing — contributes to positive change.

Unfortunately, as we know, our culture encourages consumerism, which leads to emotional isolation. Instead of turning to each other for help or fulfillment, we turn to *things*. We buy ourselves out of dilemmas instead of helping each other out. This translates into emotional isolation because good friends know each others' vulnerabilities as well as their strengths. My father carried a little poem with him all his life: "A friend is not someone who is taken in by sham. A friend is one who knows your faults, and doesn't give a damn." Fewer and fewer of us have these kinds of relationships.

The growing effort to build a collaborative culture can help change that — particularly with the new technology set up to allow people to share with each other. Websites like NeighborGoods.net, BrightNeighbor.com, or Neighborrow. com let people offer their skills and their stuff to their neighbors. Time banks let you get help for things like gardening or hair cuts or massages while you contribute time with some of your own skills.

The collaboration movement is helping solve another problem: many people work at home and miss the community of the workplace. Countering this is an initiative called *co-working*. People pay a fee to use a shared working space where they can take breaks with others and chat around the water cooler.

Sharing and the Internet

There has been a lot of negative commentary about how the Internet is cutting us off from each other, encouraging people to spend more time interacting with screens rather than with real people. And this is a serious problem — convivial gatherings like picnics and dinner parties are on the decline. But we know high tech is not going away, so we need to control it rather than let it control us. This new opportunity to promote collaboration gives us a chance to reduce the emotional isolation and the consumerism that threaten the well-being of people and the planet.

Again, even trying to describe the scope of online sharing in detail is bound to end in frustration because so many new things are happening! And the online facilitation of sharing is not only helping people build community, it's helping people survive financially. It's letting people find ways to save money or to earn a little extra money. Students have the opportunity to rent instead of buy expensive texts; people are able to rent bikes and cars cheaply; parents are exchanging kids' clothes. It's taking the shame away from renting out a room or even renting out your own car. In a real way it's giving us control over our lives because when you're a consumer, you're controlled by Madison Avenue.

Sharing and Civic Life

In March 2012, the mayor of San Francisco formed a policy group to examine the economic benefits of "the sharing economy," because many innovative companies in and around San Francisco were creating local jobs and local economic benefits. He even stressed that "every income level, across the socio-economic spectrum" was benefitting (true to the nature of sharing). "Whether it's sharing bikes, cars, apartments or tools, we must bring impacted communities and stakeholders together to develop model policies that protect public safety, reflect our values and ensure that the benefits of the 'sharing economy' extend to all San Franciscans," he said in a Shareable. net article. One of the city supervisors commented, "Peer-to-peer marketplaces are turning underutilized assets and resources into new jobs, income and community connections." Shareable Magazine publisher Neal Gorenflo said, "Sharing is a rare and practical systemic solution — it simultaneously increases access to wealth, reduces waste, and strengthens the social fabric." An action like San Francisco's demonstrates the increasing significance of the idea of sharing.

And there is a related effort that also challenges privatization — the cooperative movement. It changes the nature of our economy by encouraging workers to join together to own their own businesses, share the profit, and share in the decision making. The United Nations has made 2012 the year of the Cooperative.

Sharing and Trust

When people hear about the sharing revolution, they're very excited. But then they start to worry. What will happen if they lend out a power saw and someone gets hurt? Will the person sue? What if someone rents your car and gets in an accident.

Who pays? Attorney Janelle Orsi addresses these issues in her book, *The Sharing Solution* (2009), offering sample agreements people can use for sharing arrangements.

What's important, though, is that at last we're confronting the issue of declining trust in our culture. As trust declines, we quit believing in each other; we don't feel safe because we trust no one. And worst of all, we quit believing in democracy. Democracy means trusting in *the people*. Without democracy we will not survive because continuing with "Every man for himself" ultimately means "Last man standing."

Sharing and the Government

Ultimately, *sharing* can become a way of life. Maybe it's more a part of us than we know. For instance, let's look at the Declaration of Independence. "We hold these truths to be self-evident, that all men are created equal, that they are endowed by their Creator with certain unalienable Rights, that among these are Life, Liberty and the pursuit of Happiness. That to secure these rights, Governments are instituted among Men, deriving their just powers from the consent of the governed."

Government itself is a form of sharing. It's coming together to do things that work better together than alone. Having a fire station is a form of sharing. We can't each fight our own fires. The same with police, with roads, and on and on. Sharing is at the heart of civilized society. Maybe the sharing movement will help us understand that government itself is a way that people come together to share in the tasks that are better done together.

Maybe we'll explore *sharing* in all of its manifestations: we'll begin to see that taxes are a form of sharing the costs of taking care of a country's people. Apparently social capital — a sociological term meaning the amount of congenial interaction between people — is the best predictor of tax compliance state by state. (The best predictor of tax evasion is the number of times annually that someone gives the finger to another driver.)

Maybe the idea of sharing will help us learn to share the jobs, as they've done in Germany during the economically troubled times; share the wealth, as they've done in the Scandinavian countries, which have survived the economic troubles better than most nations; and share the power, as they've done in Denmark, a country that is one of the most equal — and happiest — countries in the world.

The Common Good

Maybe the sharing movement will help us challenge the right-wing attempts to privatize everything — from social security and medicare to schooling and health. We say we believe in life, liberty, and the pursuit of happiness, so we need to help people understand that the pursuit of happiness involves "collaborating and caring about each other," that sharing and collaborating gives us freedom from control by the corporate consumer society, that you feel truly free only when you can feel secure from worries that you will someday find yourself alone and abandoned.

Most important, the sharing movement looks so benign. Who could object to someone sharing their tools or a ladder? It doesn't *look* revolutionary. So for awhile, maybe we can fly beneath the radar, because when you start thinking about sharing, it leads to revolutionary things like participatory budgeting or cooperatives or worker-owned businesses. Ultimately sharing may be one of the most subversive things we can engage in.

Consequential Strangers

Let me open up a new slant on sharing. We know sharing helps the environment because we consume less; it helps people save money; and it builds community. But there are some hidden benefits that occurred to me as I read *Consequential Strangers*. As I mentioned earlier, talking to people as you go through your day makes you healthier and happier. But not everyone has the chance to chat with strangers or even feels comfortable doing so. *Sharing gives you that opportunity.*

When you enter the sharing revolution, you usually come in contact with strangers. Maybe you're going to a clothing exchange or a book exchange as I did. Maybe you're buying something used on Craigslist or getting rid of something on Freecycle. Maybe you're brave and are using Airbnb (renting a room in someone's house) or RelayRides (renting your car to someone you don't know). You're usually dealing with strangers.

Consequential Strangers argues that there are many more benefits to dealing with strangers than we realize. First, we often *enjoy* some of these people more than our family and friends. Why? Because we feel free. We're often stuck in certain roles with friends and families. They seldom want us to change, and we tend to conform to others' expectations. But we all have undeveloped parts of our personalities, and congenial strangers can help them emerge. Just start chatting, and you never know what new interests will come up. So sharing will give you a chance to explore new things and new aspects of yourself (a way of discovering your calling).

It reminds me of Ray Oldenburg's book *The Great Good Place* (1999). Oldenburg compares us to the chickens we buy in a typical supermarket. He says that chickens used to roam freely, pecking and exploring everything. Now they're stuffed into buildings with no room to move and put under artificial lights to make them lay more eggs. (A recent news story talked of feeding chickens caffeine so they would stay awake and lay more.) These chickens get little exercise and become stressed and diseased and are pumped full of antibiotics and hormones. Sound familiar? Like a lot people in this country.

Talking to consequential strangers is kind of like pecking and exploring freely, escaping the artificial lights of your corporate workplace. It's escaping the cages we're cooped up in, and sharing gives you the opportunity to do that.

Sharing Information

But there are practical aspects as well. We often get our information from consequential strangers. Maybe the librarian will refer you to a book you hadn't known about. Your baker may have some new recipes. The person you see at your coffee house every day might tell you about a good mechanic. The man who owns your local hardware store can suggest someone to fix your sink or even tell you how to do it yourself! You're sharing information.

This kind of information sharing certainly helps with one of the happiness factors — you feel more in control when you know the people in your neighborhood and how they can help. It gives you more people to turn to in times of emergency and crisis.

Greater Confidence

With all of this comes a new ease and self-confidence. You get used to talking with strangers, and so you feel more comfortable going to new things — classes, clubs, or political meetings. You'll know how to go up to people and get a conversation going because you get practice in the sharing culture.

Equality

My favorite part of this is that it generates equality. Chatting with strangers as you share is a great leveler — you aren't in a boss/worker role or a parent/child role. You probably don't even know much about what the other person does. You tend not to rank people based on status. You're pretty much equal.

And you step out of the consumer role, which always destroys equality and trust: who trusts a used car salesperson? When you share with people, you're a fellow human being, not a customer. They're less likely to cheat you because their reputation depends on their behavior — after an interaction, you post what happened on the Internet.

Social Cohesion

An article in *The New York Times* (May 8, 2012) talks about Repair Cafés that are being held in the Netherlands. One woman was concerned about environmental harm caused by all the stuff we throw away. So she set up a monthly informal gathering of people who could fix things and opened it to the public to bring stuff that needed to be fixed. The fixers are all volunteers and mainly older men, but everyone comes. Ironically, although it was started for sustainability reasons, it's receiving foundation money to promote "social cohesion," a program started in the wake of political murders in 2002 and 2004.

Democracy

There are two things involved in sharing that are particularly important to a democracy. As you chat amiably with people going through your day, you become more at ease with people who are different from you. A lot of racism is partly fear. When you rub shoulders with people, you fear them less. You're more flexible and open minded. Certainly much of people's acceptance of gay people came from gay people "coming out." People discovered that gays are real people with no reason to fear them.

Further, sharing evokes empathy, particularly in terms of "the stranger." When you feel at ease around others, you come to care for them. If we are ever to gain support for government social programs, we need to develop a commitment to care for people we don't know or have never seen. It's about caring what happens to the stranger. (It's strangely familiar to another story we've all heard — the good Samaritan.)

Ultimately, sharing with strangers helps you feel like you belong. This is the way to build up trust, a key ingredient in a healthy society. We trust people more when we've shared something with them; so the more people interact, the more we trust. Sharing brings you together with strangers.

The Commons as Sharing

Learning to care for strangers is an important step in caring for the common good. The idea of the common good comes to us from the idea of the *commons* — the idea that there are certain things that belong to all of us. Jay Walljasper, in his book *All*

That We Share, reminds us about the things we have in common — things like air, water, soil — and how they are being stolen from us by corporations.

Remember, at the heart of our problems of climate change, wealth inequality, wars, and on and on is the belief in the idea of "every man for himself" — that grabbing profit should be our underlying purpose. We know this doesn't work, and we're exploring things we can do to change it. In essence, we're critiquing a belief system, so we must challenge it with another belief system.

The idea of the *commons* challenges the belief system in profit and the market economy. It's the notion that there are certain things that belong to all of us and that we must learn how to manage them for the well-being of all.

Rallying for the commons is an act of resistance against the attempt to privatize everything — schools, prison, health care, social security, or water. There are certain things that people should not make profit from. The process of privatizing leads to greater wealth inequality as the owners, not the people, reap the profits.

Further, this belief in privatization leads to the idea that if something doesn't make a profit, it's not worth investing in — think of the neglected state of many public schools as well as the closing of state parks. The idea of the commons helps us resist this belief in profit that has insinuated itself into our being.

The commons also refers to the way we manage what we share. We've all heard the phrase "the tragedy of the commons"— the idea that the commons would eventually be destroyed because everyone would get what they could for themselves and ignore the interests of others. That idea has been refuted by Elinor Ostrom who, in 2009, was the first woman to receive the Nobel prize for economics. Her work, *Governing the Commons* (1990), explains how the commons can be managed for the good of everyone — essentially by involving everyone in decision making that is fair, equitable, and democratic.

We're not talking about abolishing private property. We want people to realize that private property can't exist *without* the commons — the fire fighters, the police, the court system, the military. We need not only public systems such as the police but also civic groups such as Planned Parenthood, the Sierra Club, churches, and even political parties. In fact, managing the commons is everyone's job. It's part of democracy.

A Startling New Idea

In reading about the commons, I came upon an idea that I had never heard of before. One of the writers in Walljasper's book, Peter Linebaugh, professor of history at University of Toledo, sees things like food stamps and social security as a modern expression of the commons. In other words, they're like a dividend for being a citizen and allowing the corporations to make profits from our air and water. It's similar to the Permanent Fund Dividend that all Alaskans receive each year as their share of the profits from oil. They receive, on average, between $900 and $1,800 a year, with everyone receiving the same amount. Oil is a form of the commons, and all Alaskans are benefitting from it.

This idea is significant. We've always been made to feel that food stamps are charity, and lately, even that Social Security is charity, even though we've paid into it. Linebaugh's point is that the social safety net *is the equivalent of having access to the commons.* I find this idea absolutely incredible and so logical. It's "common" sense!

In medieval days the rich people enclosed the pastures, and the Magna Carta gave back to people some of their rights to the pastures — the commons. Today, too many people are accepting the right-wing claim that there is no money for Social Security or Medicare. We need to help people understand that the social safety net is part of the commons. We have a right to it.

Similarly, in the past several years our worker productivity has skyrocketed while wages have stayed stagnant and corporate profits have soared. If we began to see the increased productivity and profit in terms of the commons, we would realize that the profit should be shared with us. Profit should be shared because we all contributed to it. It's common wealth.

The Sharing Economy

In essence, thinking in terms of the commons is another way of looking at our ultimate goal: to create a new culture in which we realize "we're all in this together." Obviously, the idea of the commons is relevant to the idea of sharing. Of course, the *sharing economy* is a more down-to-earth way to talk about a new economy. It's easier to understand what we mean when we talk about "sharing" than when we talk about "the commons."

And sharing is happening naturally — with a weak economy, people are finding that in order to survive, they need to share things. At the same time, they're discovering that they're *happier* when they share. As a result, they're questioning our competitive, consumer lifestyle, the idea that success is measured by how much you own. The idea of sharing helps people learn to think in terms of the common good. And most wonderful of all, the people who support the commons are called commoners. Now there's a word that evokes equality.

Ultimately the sharing movement is emblematic of a larger movement for a new culture that cares about the common good. It's not just collaborating in terms of our possessions, it's asking how we can collaborate in every aspect of our lives. It's saying we're "better together," and that we can't make decisions only from an individual perspective. We must get into the habit of asking how things affect everyone and not just ourselves.

This approach to life will bring us the happiness that we've discovered comes from community, calling, celebration, and control, because all of these needs are linked in the idea of sharing.

Chapter 5

Time to Talk
(Conversation, Part One)

When a friend calls to me from the road
And slows his horse to a meaning walk,
I don't stand still and look around
On all the hills I haven't hoed,
And shout from where I am, What is it?
No, not as there is a time to talk.
I thrust my hoe in the mellow ground,
Blade-end up and five feet tall,
And plod: I go up to the stone wall
For a friendly visit.

— "A Time to Talk," by Robert Frost

Reclaiming Conversation:
The Sacred Experience of Everyday Life

Joan sighed as she put down her book. She had been reading a literary history of past centuries and she wondered how people got any writing done at all. They seemed to be talking all the time, constantly engaged in conversation.

Some had actually formed conversation clubs. Emerson, Hawthorne, and Longfellow belonged to something they called the Saturday Club, and they met every week to talk about ideas and the work they were engaged in. Thoreau's family always had extra people boarding in their home, so there were lively conversations into the night. Some people even earned money from conversation; Margaret Fuller brought women together in the 19th century as paid subscribers in a gathering she called Conversations. And of course there were the French salons in the 18th century — they helped topple a government!

She sighed more deeply as she thought of her own social life. Not many good conversations these days. It was hard to make lunch dates with her friends. Sometimes they searched their calendars, only to find nothing free for weeks, and then, invariably someone would cancel because a crisis had arisen at work. And of course when there weren't any lunch dates on her calendar, she just ate at her desk, anxious to make some headway on her to-do list.

As much as she had enjoyed her evening's reading, it felt incomplete. If only she, too, could join some friends at a café and talk about what she'd read. She wondered if they still did this in Paris as much as they used to. When she visited there in her college days, she found a café in every neighborhood. Was the culture of cafés just as strong as it was when Monet, Renoir, Manet, and Degas used to gather to denounce the art establishment that refused to display their paintings? Before they were called the Impressionists they'd been called the Intransigents. Joan thought she liked that better. She could imagine the laughter and waving of arms as they decried the hypocrisy of the bourgeoisie.

Joan sighed as she went back to her book.

The Art of Conversation

Joan isn't a real person, of course. Rather, she's an amalgamation of a lot of people. Certainly the experience is real. There are a lot of people who feel like Joan, and maybe they don't even know what's bothering them. It's a vague feeling of discontent, an emptiness; and even when people recognize that something is wrong, they don't know what to do. For example, people who have been diagnosed as compulsive shoppers go to the malls not so much because they want the stuff, but because the salespeople talk to them in a friendly manner. Robert

Putnam says in *Bowling Alone* that all sorts of social interactions have dropped off — having people over for dinner, going on picnics, and playing cards have all decreased by at least 50 to 60 percent in the past 30 years.

Certainly, there is one central skill that we will need for this new culture of caring, collaboration, and concern for the common good — conversation. It's a method of change that's always been at the center of world revolutions and daily happiness.

Let's remind ourselves about why it's important. First, of course, relationships are the chief predictor of our health and well-being. John Gottman sums it up in *The Relationship Cure* (2002), saying that people with friends usually have less stress and live longer. They tend to get sick less often and recover faster when they do. One study of a group of seniors over a five-year period found that twice as many "loners" died (from all causes) as those with good friends.

And the glue that holds relationships together is conversation. Conversation is an art — an art that's been diminished in a competitive culture. We're trained to try to win in all we do. We see everything as a contest. We must learn to experience conversation as a barn raising instead of a battle. We must move away from what linguist Deborah Tannen calls *The Argument Culture* (1998).

Why is this decline happening? There are lots of reasons, but essentially, our long, stressful working hours and frenzied, aggressive lifestyles have severely reduced the chance for leisurely, positive, and supportive conversation. Not only do we spend the majority of our non-work time shopping or watching television, many of us say we are afraid to express our opinions in public, fearing a hostile or judgmental response. Too many of us have had people jump down our throats when we've spoken up; too often we've kept our mouths shut in discussions. I asked a group of people why we're afraid to speak up, and one woman said, "Because if we do, it's…" Bam! She finished her sentence by slamming her hand on the table. And lately, a lot of people are very concerned about our "plugged-in culture," with people spending more time on Facebook than on face-to-face conversation.

When I speak to groups, I often ask them to rate our conversational culture on a scale of 1 to 10, and almost everyone gives us a 2. On the surface that doesn't appear like a severe problem, yet conversation is really at the basis of almost everything important — community, democracy, world peace. It's certainly key to happiness. We need conversation for social ties; talking to new and different people helps us find our calling; being able to join in with others in a light-hearted manner helps us celebrate; and being able to express our wishes and negotiate our needs helps give us control.

Conversation is how we learn to care for each other, and maybe that's our biggest problem of all — failure to care for each other. And if we can't even care for our own species, we won't care about the rest of the species, and the health of the planet will continue to decline.

But what's going to turn things around? How can we get people to start engaging in conversation? I've been thinking about this for a long time, and I've read a lot of books that give us all sorts of techniques. The techniques are helpful, yet they don't really do the job. They don't really start a fire about conversation; they don't really get us excited. I've developed my own list of techniques, but I realized they could work only if we go deeper. It's not just a problem of conversation tips — the issue is understanding that conversation is the expression of a universal life force, an energy that flows through the universe. This sounds a little New Age-ish, but I've been very taken by the ideas of scientist/theologians Brian Swimme and Thomas Berry. They talk about the implications of the fact that the universe was formed by a fiery explosion some 15 billion years ago and has continued to emerge and evolve ever since. As Swimme says in *The Universe is a Green Dragon* (1984), "Everything that exists is involved in this emergence— galaxies and stars and planets and light and all living creatures." They see an underlying life force, a guiding energy that continues to flow through the universe. And human beings are the latest evolutionary expression of the Energy.

This means that what we say — communicate — is the expression of this vast universal intelligence. Some people, both scientists and religious people, might object to this, thinking it's either too religious or not religious enough. Most of us, though, rejected our childhood religions because what they taught wasn't compatible with what we learned in our science classes. But I think as a people we have discovered that rejecting religion doesn't mean that the basic human impulse for connection, meaning, and joy has left us. What we want is an experience of exuberance and transcendence — an experience of ecstasy and delight and a feeling that we belong to something larger than ourselves. The problem is, our sense of life has been diminished, reduced to the trivial and mundane. Nothing has any real importance.

But once upon a time it did. I remember how it felt when I was a little girl. When my parents would go to someone's house for dinner, my mother would not leave me at home with a babysitter. No, she'd take me along. I would listen to the adults talk while we had dinner, and when I got tired I would fall asleep next to the coats on the bed, listening to the comforting sound of adult voices engaged in conversation.

And I've certainly had wonderful conversations in my life. Just recently, as a matter of fact. A friend of my husband was visiting. We'd known him for a long time, but that night we got to know him better and made real contact. He was going through a divorce; his teenage daughter had been having problems; and a love affair had just blown up. He was trying to figure out what to do. Further, his lover wanted him to go to a drug treatment program because he smoked pot. He didn't tell us all this as a sob story, with a "woe is me" tone. No, he wanted help in figuring out what to do. He asked us questions — whether we thought a marriage really needed passion, how many soul mates people would have in their lives. Things like that. It was a wonderful evening of conversation.

Now, you're thinking that we don't all have such compli-cated and intense lives to talk about. But in a way we do. We just seem scared to talk to people about what's really going on in our lives. We go to therapists and counselors instead and keep up a good front for our friends. I've had friends tell me they were getting a divorce and I hadn't had an inkling that anything was wrong.

Maybe one of the reasons our friend could talk to us like he did is that I've come to the decision that I will live my life com-mitted to the idea that we are each an expression of that early fiery explosion, and that each conversation is a significant event that allows us to experience that cosmic flow of energy. Some people might talk about this in different terms and think of this life force as God or the Tao. But I don't think the words mat-ter. It is simply an acknowledgment, I think, that when we see life as just a bunch of random accidents that have no purpose beyond our limited selves, then life isn't worth living. No one can prove that there is a guiding energy, an ultimate reality, a universal mind, but I've decided that the odds are good enough for me, and that rekindling conversation is a way to experience the exuberance and transcendence of something larger.

Many have grappled with finding the right words for a sacred experience, and those words seem relevant to the idea of conversation. Alan Jones, once a dean of Grace Cathedral, calls spirituality "the art of making connections." Brother David Steindl-Rast, a Benedictine monk, says that spirituality is when one feels alive. "Wherever we come alive, that is the area in which we are spiritual .... To be vital, awake, aware, in all areas of our lives, is the task that is never accomplished, but it remains the goal." Abraham Heschel defines spirituality as "the reference to the transcendent in our own existence, the direction of the Here toward the Beyond. It is the ecstatic force that stirs all our goals .... When we perceive it, it is as if our mind were gliding for a while with an eternal current."

Deciding to act on those words has changed the way I look at everything. If we are expressions of this "eternal thou," as

Jewish theologian Martin Buber expressed it, then conversations take on an ultimate importance. Each conversation is an expression of the eternal thou in each one of us. Each conversation allows our real selves to emerge and gives us a chance to help the real self of the other emerge. Laughter becomes a form of sacred energy that expands and lifts us up. I don't like any of the religious or spiritual words, so I've come only to think of what I mean as connectedness.

What I felt as a child lying beside the coats, what I felt with our friend going through a divorce, was part of the same experience — a deep connectedness. It is a belief in a creative energy flowing through all of life, a life force, an interdependent web of existence in which we must exuberantly, not grimly, participate. Theologian Matthew Fox says that we live in a time of acedia, a time of "not caring" — we have no passion, no energy, and we suffer from ennui, listlessness, apathy, indifference, dullness. Eventually acedia becomes despair, hopelessness, and nihilism, causing us to experience what Robert Lifton talks about when he describes Hiroshima survivors — psychic numbing. I think that many of our experiences of conversation reflect these feelings of apathy and indifference. Expanding our concept of life will help us break through this conversational deadness.

Transformative Techniques: Conversation as the Sacred Expression of the True Self

The highest revelation is that God is in every man.
— Ralph Waldo Emerson

I've found that when I look at conversation as the expression of the eternal thou or the unfolding of the universe, my experience of conversation is much different. When I express my self, I am expressing an infinite self. But just having an abstract idea isn't enough. We need to remember the transformative conversations we've had in our past and learn from them.

I remember a talk with my high school English teacher, Mr. Lander. Every Friday we had book reports. He had the class sit quietly and read while we went to his desk individually to talk about the books we'd read. On one of those days Mr. Lander and I talked about Sinclair Lewis' *Main Street*, and he said something that helped set the course of my life. He told me he thought I was a lot like the protagonist in *Main Street*, the young woman who wanted to change things in that small, provincial town with its narrow ideas and prejudices. I remember thinking, "Yes, he's right!" I felt thrilled that he had recognized that in me.

Looking back, I see what a gift that conversation was. He saw the core of my being, someone no one else had really recognized, or at least talked with me about. This seems to me to be the true role of conversation — to bring out the essence of the other person, to affirm that essence, to help figure out how to express it. Sometimes you might help the person discover a sense of self as my teacher did, and sometimes you might engage in problem solving in the face of a life decision. I remember the time I walked around the lake that I live near in Seattle, talking with a friend. (There's something about walking and talking in nature that brings an aliveness and clarity. I like to think that we all — my friend and I and the trees and flowers and the water — are caught up in a larger conversation, that we have opened ourselves to some sort of transcendent energy flowing through the universe.) That particular day I was trying to decide whether to continue as a community college administrator (which brought me little joy or exuberance) or to quit and teach classes in community settings — become a "community educator." I remember her words: "Cecile, why don't you think of your community teaching as your form of art, and artists are always willing to suffer for their art?" Of course! What a wonderful way to see ourselves — as artists, regardless of what we do. More than anyone, the artist seems to participate in this energy flow. That conversation helped me make a decision, and I resigned (with nary a regret).

And so, conversations have helped me stay in touch not only with other people but with myself. And they continue to. For the past several months I've once again been engaged in significant conversations — this time with two friends talking about the meaning and purpose of life. Instead of walking the lake, we meet in our living rooms with cups of tea — maybe not calling up the spirit of nature, but perhaps calling up the spirit of women in the past who gathered around the hearth and stitched quilts or shelled peas. We talk about our plans and ideas and realize anew with each conversation how liberating and affirming and inspiring these conversations are. In these conversations I feel total unconditional goodwill radiating from the other two women, something I rarely feel in our commercialized, competitive society. But it's something we need if we are going to risk expressing our true selves.

All of these conversations have helped me participate in the energy I feel flowing through life, to feel more alive and connected to all of life. But ultimately, it isn't easy. I think we have to commit ourselves to experiencing conversation in this way. The sentence that keeps running through my mind is from the former freedom fighter and later president of Czechoslovakia, Vaclav Havel, who died in 2011: "Each person somehow succumbs to a profound trivialization of his or her inherent humanity." Somehow our sense of what is possible for us in life has been severely diminished. Sixties activist Tom Hayden talks about the diminishment of our lives. He said that we live with less because all we've ever known is less. We don't understand how important it is to express our true selves, and we fail to realize that conversation is the most basic way to do it. Thus, we allow the significance of conversation to be trivialized and ignored. Conversation is seen only as a workhorse and never as a magnificent horse racing free over the plains. It exists mainly to transact business, to pass on information — instead of a way to experience exuberance and transcendence.

The first step, then, is understanding the vital significance of conversation. But then we have to take the leap and try it out and prove to ourselves how vital good conversation is. Once we experience the delight and joy of good conversation, we will work to rekindle it. How, then, do we go about having conversations of more depth and aliveness?

I want to discuss the techniques that I've found to be helpful. But we have to be careful. Remember when we were told to practice "active listening"? The idea was good, but it became too pat, too mechanical. We were told to make sure to listen and rephrase what the other was saying, but instead of sounding sincere and caring, we just sounded manipulative. In fact, focusing only on conversational techniques can become manipulative: People would say, "What I think I hear you saying ..." and then they would proceed to twist your words beyond all recognition.

Periodically we have to remind ourselves of what we want and need from conversation.

- We want to be recognized for who we are, to feel that the other person has discovered our true essence, that she or he has fallen in love with our true selves.
- We want to feel valued, affirmed, cared for, and enjoyed.
- We want to be heard and appreciated.
- We want to be respected.
- We want to feel enthusiastic and absorbed.
- We want to feel fascination for the topic of conversation and affection for the other person.
- We want to feel that we are learning and growing and discovering ourselves, that new possibilities are being opened to us.
- We want to discover what we have in common with others, and we want to discover our uniqueness.
- We want to leave a conversation feeling more excited about life, more confident about ourselves.
- We want to feel that we have discovered more fully who we are, that we see more clearly our passions and vocation.
- We want to feel that we have taken a risk and revealed ourselves, that we have reached out and made contact.
- We want exuberance and transcendence.

- And at the same time, we want all of this for the other person as well.

Practicing the Art of Conversation: Some Things to Remember

There are three basic things I like to remember when I converse with someone:

- I try to remember that this is a sacred encounter and that I want the universe to help me make a profound contact with the other person.
- I remind myself to look for what I can learn from the other person.
- I ask myself how I can help the other person feel more affirmed, more understood, more valued.

Here are the things that seem to me to be important if we are to have conversations of exuberance and transcendence.

Number One: Take the Risk of Saying What You Think or Feel

Say what you know, do what you must, come what may.

— Sonya Kovalevsky, 19th-century mathematician

In 1929, two Oxford dons began talking. As C. S. Lewis wrote to a friend, "I was up till 2:30 on Monday, talking to the Anglo Saxon professor Tolkien, who came back with me to college from a society and sat discoursing of the gods and giants of Asgard for three hours, then departing in the wind and rain — who could turn him out, for the fire was bright and the talk good." Apparently Tolkien had always been fascinated with Nordic epics and had been working on one of his own since he was eighteen, but he had allowed only one person to see it — an old mentor who had advised him to drop it. It wasn't the sort of thing that would further one's academic career.

But after discovering their shared interests in Nordic issues, Tolkien gave Lewis one of the unfinished poems to read. Lewis wrote back saying that he had sat up late the night before to read it and it gave him "an evening of delight." That encouraged Tolkien to read aloud his work to Lewis, and gradually a small group of friends (who called themselves the Inklings because they dabbled in ink and had vague intimations and ideas) gathered to read their work to each other. Over the next several years they developed a regular meeting time on Thursday nights in Lewis's room in Magdalen College. Tolkien, of course went on to publish *The Hobbit* and *The Lord of the Rings*.

The relationship between Tolkien and Lewis changed Lewis as well. Lewis was attracted to Christianity, but Oxford dons tended to sneer at religions, so Lewis didn't reveal his interests. But one night, Tolkien and Lewis and another friend stayed up until three in the morning talking about Christianity, and gradually the Inklings began to focus on it — freeing Lewis to go on and publish many books on Christianity.

In his diary, Tolkien wrote that the "friendship with Lewis compensates for much and besides giving constant pleasure and comfort has done me much good from the contact with a man at once honest, brave, intellectual, a scholar, a poet, and a philosopher." Many years later, Tolkien wrote of Lewis, "The unpayable debt I owe to him was not influence as it is usually understood, but sheer encouragement. He was for long my only audience. Only from him did I ever get the idea that my stuff could be more than a private hobby."

What I find remarkable in this story is two things: One, how important it was for these talented, creative men to have the support of a group, and two, the courage it took each one of them to speak up in the first place. The groups would never have formed if someone had not reached out, invited someone else to a café to talk.

Now, perhaps you're thinking, "They were artists. What have I got to talk to people about?" Ultimately, we each need to see ourselves as artists, and our art form is our words. We must feel the same urgent need to express our unique vision as artists do. Usually it will be in little, seemingly unimportant ways. What did you really think of the movie — even if you disagree with the anointed critics? Do you have the courage to risk the sneers of the English majors by saying that you like to read John Grisham? Can you risk telling a friend that you've begun writing haiku? Again, these don't seem like big things, but unless we can be true to ourselves in the little, everyday ways, we won't be able to stand up for the important issues of the day.

I was at a dinner party the other night when a man, a very quiet man who rarely reveals much about himself, said he had spent the previous weekend at a meditation retreat. It wasn't an earthshaking revelation, but I don't think it was easy for him to talk about it. He was probably thinking, "Wow, they'll think I'm a flake, or they'll think I'm a hypocrite." But by being willing to say something with depth and to reveal something important about himself, the man brought greater depth to our conversation.

It's hard to say what you think when you know no one else agrees with you — when you're pro-choice and you know everyone in the group is anti-choice, or when you disagree with the president's foreign policy and everyone else in the room supports it. In these cases, just listening to the other person may be the most important thing to do. You might say, "Well, I don't share all your views, but I'm really anxious to try to understand what you feel and think."

When you say what you think or feel, you're acting as a conduit for the wisdom of the universe. Each time you express your true self, you're making contact with the universe. But each time you reveal your real self, you take a tremendous risk. It's hard to get over the fear that you'll make a fool of yourself, that people will think you're stupid, that you're crazy. Yet you must do it. You never know what will come of it.

Number Two: Listen

Listening is a magnetic and strange thing, a creative force…. When we are listened to, it creates us, makes us

unfold and expand. Ideas actually begin to grow within
us and come to life.... When we listen to people there is
an alternating current, and this recharges us so that we
never get tired of each other ... and it is this little creative
fountain inside us that begins to spring and cast up new
thoughts and unexpected laughter and wisdom.... Well,
it is when people really listen to us, with quiet fascinated
attention, that the little fountain begins to work again,
to accelerate in the most surprising way.

— Brenda Ueland

Holy listening— to "listen" another's soul into life,
into a condition of disclosure and discovery, may
be almost the greatest service that any human being
ever performs for another.

— Douglas Steere, Quaker

The more faithfully you listen to the voice within you,
the better you will hear what is sounding outside.
And only he who listens can speak.

— Dag Hammarskjold

There is a guidance for each of us, and by lowly listening
we shall hear the right word.... Place yourself in the middle
of the stream of power and wisdom which flows into
your life. Then, without effort, you are impelled to
truth and to perfect contentment.

— Ralph Waldo Emerson

One day, a man said to me, "Cecile, I've been wondering what you think about …." I don't remember what he asked about, but I remember I loved the question. How incredible for someone to ask your opinion. How wonderful to know someone wants to hear what you have to say.

Listening is at the heart of conversation. Don't worry about saying anything important or witty yourself — remember that the act of listening can be the most important thing in the world. When we begin to see conversation as a way to bring into being our own as well as another person's unique expression of the universe, the act of listening takes on tremendous significance.

It sounds obvious to say that listening is the most basic thing we can do in conversation. But I think we all realize how seldom we really get listened to. I've had too many conversations in which it appears that the other person is listening — at least ceasing to talk while I'm speaking — but so often the other person just starts up where he or she left off, with no reference to anything I said. It's always the strangest sensation, as though there are two people in a room just making random comments that have nothing to do with each other.

So I, who am an easy talker, try to remember that each conversation can be a sacred, life-transforming experience, and I remind myself that listening is the most important thing I can be doing, and then I try to pay full attention.

Usually that means doing nothing but listening, looking into the other's eyes. Of course, there are times that we'll talk while we work — while we're fixing dinner together, chopping vegetables or stirring a sauce, or while we're cleaning up, washing and drying the dishes together. We're doing something else, but we're paying attention to what the other person says. In fact, these kinds of activities can be conducive to conversation because we lose our self-consciousness. But this is different from those times when you visit in an office and the other person just keeps working or fiddling with things on the desk, checking the clock as if waiting for something more important to happen.

To learn to listen better, I've tried to learn not to jump in immediately when someone else takes a breath but to say things like, "My goodness," "How interesting," or even "Tell me more." It's important to nod and maybe mirror the other's emotions — smile in response to a smile, frown in response to a frown. It's the non-verbal way of affirming what the other is saying.

This doesn't mean you just sit in silence. Part of listening is responding — probably with a sympathetic story that happened to you. If the other person has taken the risk to reveal the self, maybe you should too. (It depends on how well you want to know the person. Personal revelation is a gift and shouldn't be given to everyone.)

Listening is wider than just the interpersonal experience. It begins with listening to one's self. Even though our frenzied lives don't leave us much time, the place to begin is by taking time each day to just sit in silence. Or take a walk without speakers stuck in your ears. It doesn't need to be a formal meditation — just sit and watch what emerges. Think of it as having a conversation with yourself — listening to the still, small, inner voice.

As we begin to see ourselves as an expression of the energy of the universe, we see the importance of listening to that voice. Part of this is listening to one's own life, to the lessons of life. In our culture we learn that life is a series of random events that we have chosen, that we have decided on. Some of us, the privileged, see ourselves climbing the ladder of success. We congratulate ourselves for our intelligence, attractiveness, and superiority. But throughout history, there has been another view, people have seen themselves as being called, or led. And so they search their experiences to understand what the soul of the universe is trying to teach them. This kind of listening to one's self leads to finding one's calling, an essential part of happiness.

Number Three: Be Congenial

> *It is a bit embarrassing to have been concerned with*
> *the human problem all one's life and find at the end*
> *that one has no more to offer by way of advice than*
> *"try to be a little kinder."*
> — Aldous Huxley

> *Oh, the comfort — the inexpressible comfort of feeling*
> *safe with a person, having neither to weigh thoughts nor*

*measure words, but pouring them all right out, just as they
are, chaff and grain together, certain that a faithful hand
will take and sift them, keep what is worth keeping and
then with a breath of kindness blow the rest away.*

— George Eliot

Always say things in a way that encourages others to say what
they think or feel. Help others to discover their own truths
while you try to express yours.

When you say that you didn't like a movie, you don't have to
imply that anyone who liked it was an idiot — which is what
usually happens. I was at a meeting of a group the other day
in which no one really talked to each other, they just spent the
time giving their opinions, advocating for their particular causes.
If someone had a different viewpoint, an argument emerged as
they attacked each others' ideas. One person said something
about her pet snake and another person immediately responded
by saying she thought it was wrong to have pets of any kind. This
isn't a good conversation. No one is really making any contact at
all. It was like people were fencing, but totally missing each time
they jabbed their swords — they were just poking empty air.

I've found it helpful to preface my opinions with statements like "It seems to me ..." or "In my experience ..." and
end my sentences with "What do you think?" I'm telling others
that I don't think that only my viewpoint is correct and that
I'm anxious to hear what they have to say.

This assumes a different view of truth than the one we're
taught in schools — where we are graded on our answers and
told we're right or wrong. Most of us have been brought up to
think of truth in terms of facts or information — something
that can be proven or checked. True or false: 3 plus 3 is 7? We
know, of course, that the answer is false. This is the limited
view of truth we've learned. I'm suggesting that in the larger
questions of life we each have a bit of the truth, and that we
can learn from each other's experience — no need to try to
swat others' ideas down. Seen this way, truth is the authentic

expression of self and therefore people's different experiences can all be true. A person who grows up on welfare will have a different experience of life than someone who grows up with a comfortable lifestyle. Each person's experience is valid.

This vision of truth means that we're always searching for truth, that our opinions are only tentative, that we're always open to new information and revisions of our ideas. If we remember that we are an expression of an evolving universe and that change is one of the essential facts of life, we'll try to resist becoming doctrinaire and rejecting others' ideas. If we only argue with others — try to prove them wrong — we aren't open to learning from others, and we close ourselves off from growth. This means that when I listen to someone else's expression of truth, I hope that my sense of truth is expanded and changed. I am expanded.

Truth can be discovered through conversation, and so, when we speak with people, it's not only important that we listen, but that we express ourselves in ways that invite them to continue to express their truths.

Number Four: Speak with Enthusiasm and Energy

> *Everything can be taken from us but one thing — the*
> *last of the human freedoms — to choose one's attitude*
> *in any given circumstance.*
>
> — Viktor Frankl, Jewish philosopher and
> concentration camp survivor

The other night I went to listen to a panel, and the people who spoke sounded as though they were just about to die, as if they had only enough energy to crawl home. They had decided to give their talks sitting down — I guess so that they would seem more egalitarian — but they just seemed like they were about 150 years old.

I've never understood why people switch into such dull personae when they get up in front of people. Do they think that it makes them sound more intelligent? Is the academic world so mistrustful of emotions that we have been taught to squelch feelings, turning us into deadly bores?

Start watching. Most people sound as though they couldn't care less when they talk. Maybe it's just a habit or it's because we unconsciously imitate others' way of speech — which we do, of course — but to be a good conversationalist, you have to be enthusiastic. Get excited about something. When did we learn that we need to be cool? I think it's fear about what others think, so we won't show our real selves, and maybe it's endemic to a competitive society where we've been taught to win, to not be real. You learn to play your cards close to your chest, revealing nothing.

Maybe we're afraid to express enthusiasm because we think people will laugh and think we're foolish. But if we think of life as experiencing the flow of the universe, we have to dive in with energy. Enthusiasm means being open to experiencing and expressing the energy of the universe, and we become a weak connection if we hold ourselves back. Ralph Waldo Emerson said, "Nothing great was ever achieved without enthusiasm. The way of life is wonderful; it is by abandonment." Louis Pasteur said, "The Greeks have given us one of the most beautiful words of our language, the word 'enthusiasm' — a God within. The grandeur of the acts of men is measured by the inspiration from which they spring. Happy is he who bears a God within."

Of course, we don't want a false gaiety. Sometimes you'll be talking about things you're not happy about, so enthusiasm isn't the quality we want — maybe better words are energy or passion. When I hear people on television speaking about awful things in flat, expressionless voices, I wonder what it does to our emotional response. Does it deaden it?

Sometimes I hold back because I fear I will overwhelm people, but accommodating for that doesn't mean we have to be bland. We want to be real without closing down the other person, but we don't want to be colorless and dull. Maybe we need to have the courage to be an eccentric. I've always liked Thoreau's thoughts on this:

> Men are very generally spoiled by being so civil and well-disposed. You can have no profitable conversation with them, they are so conciliatory, determined to agree with you. They exhibit such long-suffering and kindness in a short interview. I would meet with some provoking strangeness, so that we may be guest and host and refresh one another. It is possible for a man wholly to disappear and be merged in his manners. The thousand and one gentlemen whom I meet, I meet despairingly and but to part from them, for I am not cheered by the hope of any rudeness from them. A cross man, a coarse man, an eccentric man, a silent, a man who does not drill well — of him there is some hope. Your gentlemen, they are all alike. They utter their opines as if it was not a man that uttered them. It is "just as you please"; they are indifferent to everything. They will talk with you for nothing. The interesting man will rather avoid [you], and it is a rare chance if you get so far as talk with him. The laborers whom I know, the loafers, fishers, and hunters, I can spin yarns with profitably, for it is hands off; they are they and I am I still.... I am never electrified by my gentleman; he is not an electric eel, but one of the common kind that slip through your hands, however hard you clutch them, and leave them covered with slime.

Number Five: Appreciate Others

> *The deepest principle in human nature is the craving to be appreciated.*
> — William James

> *The world is so empty if one thinks only of mountains, rivers and cities; but to know someone who thinks and feels*

with us, and who, though distant, is close to us in spirit,
this makes the earth for us an inhabited garden.

— Goethe

Man wishes to be confirmed in his being by man, and
wishes to have a presence in the being of the other.

— Martin Buber

In 1986 Sigmund Freud wrote to a friend, "Your kind should not die out, my dear friend, the rest of us need people like you too much. How much I owe you: solace, understanding, stimulation in my loneliness, meaning to my life that I gained through you, and finally even health that no one else could have given back to me. It is primarily through your example that intellectually I gained the strength to trust my judgment, even when I am left alone — though not by you .... I know that you do not need me as much as I need you, but I also know that I have a secure place in your affection."

It's incredible to read these words. Who today would say something like that to a friend? Would we even think it? How would we feel if we received such a message? How would we feel if we sent such a message ourselves?

A friend of mine told me that at his elite university the first five minutes of talking with people were spent in "image management," trying subtly to work in all your recent awards and honors, communicating how important you are. I've always liked the quip, "Well, enough about me! Let's talk about you! What did you think of my latest book?" After such an exchange, you walk away exhausted, feeling empty and isolated.

So pay attention to the other person. We need to respond with phrases such as "What an interesting idea!" "What a good point!" "How true!" "I think you've got something there." Certainly we don't want to feign enthusiasm, but when you feel glad to see someone, express it in your voice. I actually try to use those phrases a lot, but I really feel that I hardly ever hear them from someone else.

Try, when you've been with someone awhile, to reflect back to them their unique qualities. Say things like, "You seem to me like the kind of person who's really good at understanding people." "It seems to me that you have a special gift for solving conflicts." "I've noticed that you are very persuasive when you feel strongly about something." Don't make anything up, just try to capture what you find is important about the other person.

Number Six: Ask Good Questions

> *You can tell whether a man is clever by his answers.*
> *You can tell whether a man is wise by his questions.*
>
> — Naguib Mahfouz

"When in your life did you experience community?" It's a question I like to ask in my workshops and then have the students gather in small groups to tell their stories. I hear stories of people helping each other in earthquakes, stories about long nights of talking during college dorm life, stories about friendships formed on daily bus rides. I like to stand back and just steep myself in the rising noise and laughter as people delve into their memories.

The quality of your conversation depends on the kinds of questions you ask. You can start with questions like "How did you like the movie?" But you need to probe deeper and ask why they liked it. Ask them what they actually felt — fear, connection, amazement? I've found that the best kinds of questions are about people's pasts. Ask them what they were like as kids. People really open up when you do that. One of my favorite conversationalists says things like, "Peter, you've always been really good about helping others. I wonder how you developed that ability." And the other person almost always responds in a way that is profoundly moving, usually with a story from his or her past.

Always try to move past ideas to feelings. When someone tells me something, I try to ask, "How did you feel about that?"

"Did you feel good about that?" When talking about books or movies, I want people to tell me which character they identified with; I want to know the other person better. I try to move from the simple question about information (Did you like the movie?) to one focusing on feeling (How did it make you feel?) and then to an analytic question. (I wonder why you felt that way.)

Number Seven: Be an Equal

> *There is nothing that exasperates people more than a*
> *display of superior ability or brilliance in conversation.*
> *They seem pleased at the time, but their envy makes*
> *them curse the conversationalist in their heart.*
>
> — Samuel Johnson

When I was writing my dissertation for my doctorate, my husband would sometimes hear me talking to my advisor. Afterwards he would tell me, "You sounded like you were about ten years old." When I talked to her my brain froze up and I stammered and stumbled over my words. It was because there was such a status gap between the professor and the student (although she could have done something more to overcome it).

You can't have a good conversation unless you present yourself as an equal. Studies have found that there are certain factors in a conversation that indicate one's status. The person who has the greater status generally spends the most time talking and the lower-status person spends more time listening. Further, the lower-status person spends more time laughing at the other's clever comments as well as revealing more personal information. So notice what's happening when you're talking to people. Don't play the role of the inferior or the superior.

And even though listening is key to a good conversation, you should really have a back and forth, building on each others' responses. Don't just let the other person go on and on. Conversation should be a participatory, reciprocal activity. Listening and drawing the other person out may draw people to you, but I think you'll grow resentful if you don't get to talk as well.

Of course, creating equality in conversation is not easy to do. It's as though we give ourselves points when we walk into a room: "Well, that person has more education than I do, but I'm more attractive than she is." "That person loses points because he's too young, and the person beside him loses points because he's too old."

But when we remember that we are all expressions of the evolving universe, of the life force, we know that we are all equals, and that each of us has something important to express.

Number Eight: Tell Your Own Stories

> *We do not talk — we bludgeon one another with facts*
> *and theories gleaned from cursory readings of newspapers,*
> *magazines and digests.*
>
> — Henry Miller

> *I was born into a storytelling family and wrote my*
> *first story when I was five years old, and have been*
> *writing and reading stories ever since because the story*
> *is the human being's chief vehicle of truth.*
>
> — Madeleine L'Engle

> *We have stories to tell, stories that provide wisdom about*
> *the journey of life. What more have we to give one another*
> *than our "truth" about our human adventure as honestly*
> *and as openly as we know how?*
>
> — Rabbi Saul Rubin

I was at a dinner party not long ago where we started discussing a standard academic question: Why aren't there more women in the sciences? We discussed the theories of the experts until we almost put ourselves to sleep. Then, one woman told the story of how it felt when she was the only woman in a class and the men ignored her jokes. And how it felt when the men just talked about machines — any kind of machine: motor boats, lawn mowers, cars, computers. We all remembered similar stories, and as we told them, we laughed and laughed.

It was the story, not just the ideas, that made the conversation come alive. You need them both. When you only give opinions or talk about facts, you risk getting into a competitive discussion, with the better informed or more highly educated person coming out ahead. When you tell a story, you establish yourself as an equal because being better educated is no guarantee of being a better storyteller (often the opposite, in fact). Stories move you beyond facts and figures into feelings and emotions, and help you connect.

I try to start out with a story that lets me set a tone for the conversation by modeling an open and participatory approach. I want people to know that they don't have to worry about impressing me or arguing with me. I want to signal that I'm not playing any competitive games. A good way to start is to tell a story that reveals some of your own vulnerabilities and shortcomings. Tell about a time you made a fool of yourself! (Too many people just recount the good things that happen, and everyone starts resenting them.) I always like to tell people about the time I was trying to impress a dignitary at lunch only to discover I'd been dunking my French dip sandwich in my coffee. Or about the time when I wore my jacket inside out to a fancy wedding. When you tell those stories and laugh at yourself, you make others feel comfortable to laugh with you. And then they can drop their guard and tell their stories.

Stories draw us together. Some of the best times are recalling shared stories and searching them together for meaning. Not long ago I enjoyed a conversation involving several of us who had worked at the same community college. We started talking about why the women presidents never lasted long, and then we expanded to talking about leadership in general. The conversation could have deteriorated into just saying nasty things about others, but we were genuinely trying to answer some basic life questions about leadership and the differences between men and women. It was a very creative, satisfying conversation.

When you tell stories together you are carrying on a tradition that is as old as humanity. Stories are central to the human existence because we are trying to figure out our own stories, searching for the themes that tell us who we are and what our purpose is.

Number Nine: Laugh Freely

> *In conversation, humor is worth more than wit and easiness more than knowledge.*
>
> — George Herbert

There's a story recounted by Robert Drennan, in his book *The Algonquin Wits*, about Franklin Pierce Adams and George and Beatrice Kaufman, members of the roundtable at the Algonquin Hotel, along with Dorothy Parker, Robert Benchley, and Robert Sherwood. One evening Adams and the Kaufmans were at a dinner party, and Beatrice Kaufman sat on a cane-bottom chair and broke through the seat. There she was, stuck, with her feet in the air, her derriere firmly wedged. Adams looked at her and, instead of hurrying over to help her out and avoid further embarrassment, he said, "Beatrice, I've told you a hundred times, that's not funny!"

What a gift to respond like that. You can imagine that the embarrassed silence was undermined by a burst of laughter. Nothing frees people like laughing. Nothing connects people like laughing together. The stresses of the day are released and life looks a little more promising and you feel lighter and somehow more free. It helps if you can become an easy laugher yourself. Don't hold back. If you're out of practice, read funny things or watch funny movies. If you laugh at your own jokes, people almost always join in.

And when we laugh, it's not just about superficial things. I remember the thrill of sitting in an early feminist consciousness-raising group, talking about marriage and children and the meaning of life. I remember the incredible feeling of telling the truth about my life and discovering that I wasn't alone in my discontent. But most of all I remember our laughter. The stories we told in that early women's circle were about the ridiculous things in our lives — about dressing wrong or tripping in a public place. We even laughed about marrying the wrong person or about our husbands leaving us.

Laughter took the sting from our memories. Laughing, it seems to me, is the expression that life is wonderful, that even though we suffer, it's all worth it. It's a gesture of liberation, thumbing our noses at the powers of oppression, saying that we refuse to give in, that we believe in ourselves and in our own freedom and equality. When we laugh at ourselves, at the times we made fools of ourselves, we break down barriers between people because they see that we don't take ourselves too seriously. When we laugh at ourselves we affirm that we believe in the essential equality of all people, that no one is more important than anyone else. When people laugh together, they become equals and experience connectedness. Laughter comes close to being a sacred experience — a time when one feels the most delight and enthusiasm about being alive. (And of course health research backs me up: people who laugh a lot have longer and healthier lives.)

And think of how laughter has been trivialized — the ubiquitous laugh track, a machine that mimics this sacred experience. Or how laughter has been driven out of our lives — would you dare sit around laughing in the workplace? It is in conversation that you experience the most delightful, freeing laughter. That's where you can laugh yourself sick, where the more you laugh, the more joyful and wonderful life becomes.

Number Ten: Experience Life as an Adventure

> *Life is either a grand adventure or nothing.*
> — Helen Keller

One of my favorite conversationalists is someone who travels a lot. He doesn't necessarily talk about his travels, but I think it's helped make him a good conversationalist because it's kept his curiosity and enthusiasm alive. But really, it's symbolic. We have to see life as an incredible journey, as an adventure. If you have an interesting life, you will tend to be interesting conversationalist, but we just don't do much that is interesting. We spend the majority of our time outside of work commuting, watching television, grazing in the malls, or visiting Facebook. What's there to talk about?

We're protected from most of the elements; if we're cold we touch a little button to adjust the temperature — we don't chop wood and build a fire. When we go on a trip, climbing into a car is nothing like getting on a horse or into a horse-drawn buggy. I remember once, when I was leading a youth program in the deep South, my co-leader decided it would be instructive to have the kids kill a chicken for their dinner. Believe me, it was certainly more interesting than buying a package of cellophane-wrapped chicken — if you call a headless, bloody chicken running around interesting. I know that few of us would trade modern conveniences for some of the old practices, but we haven't replaced them with anything vital, and so our conversation is dull.

That may be starting to change, though, in the "reskilling" classes groups such as the Transition movement offers. In fact, one woman told a story about how she went to a solar cooking class and part of the instruction was learning how to kill a chicken in a kinder fashion than we used to do. Not only was the conversation interesting, it turned out to be really funny as people started recalling the way their grandmothers had killed chickens — swinging them around by their necks, and using other picturesque methods.

So we need to search for real, vital experiences. But even if our lives are not highly exciting, we can take action to deepen our experience. We can go to more lectures and museums. Join groups like Transition. Go on demonstrations. Volunteer to work in a homeless shelter not just because it's a civic duty but because life will be more interesting and we'll have more to converse about and as a result, life will get even more interesting. Watch foreign movies. Go on flash mobs. If we expose ourselves to life, we'll have something to talk about.

If we all think the same, hear the same television broadcasts, we grow dull. Dull people can't have vivid conversations.

Number Eleven: Talk randomly

> *Listening to people talking I could enter into their lives,*
> *feel their tattered clothes on my back, walk with my*
> *feet in their shoes; their desires, their needs, all passed*
> *into my soul, or my soul passed into theirs.*
>
> — Honoré de Balzac

I once heard a woman say that when she was single and hoping to meet a man, she read a book that said she had to talk to five new men a day. So she did it, even though it was hard, and she ended up marrying someone that she met this way.

We should each take that pledge. Commit to talking to five new people a day. We always learn by doing. We learn to converse by talking with people. (And then, of course, we get more good stories, because interesting things are bound to happen.)

But interacting with people gets to be more and more difficult. The doctor no longer makes house calls or really gets to know the patient — a patient gets a few minutes with the doctor, a bunch of tests are done, and some pills prescribed. Or if something is really serious, the patient is sent to a specialist who focuses only on a specific part of the body and assigns a series of tests that other people carry out with their machines.

Few of us have a corner mom-and-pop grocery store where we know the owners and they know us and we can chat. We shop in discount stores where there is a new face every time we go because the pay is so low there's tremendous turnover. But, with the rise of "localization," that's changing. I have some of my best conversations with people as I go out on my daily walk, stopping in the book store, the grocery co-op, and the library. *Consequential Strangers* shows that talking to a wide variety of people can help us develop new interests and new aspects of ourselves. Our friends and family rarely want us to change, so if we're with only them, there will be little new in our lives and we'll become less interesting and maybe even less creative.

We tend to get our money out of machines; our phones are answered by machines; we spend our days sending messages through a machine. Go into the bank and deal with the teller. Press zero on your phone to get the receptionist. Look at it as a project to keep down unemployment. Call someone instead of sending an email. And talk with them. Some of my nicest times are three-minute chats with a person on the street selling a newspaper for a homeless project. Talking randomly not only makes you happier but healthier as well.

As a culture we have to learn, as Robert Frost's person did in the opening poem, to stop and take a "time to talk."

Chapter 6

Time to Talk
(Conversation, Part Two)

It takes two to speak the truth — one to speak,
and another to hear.

— Henry David Thoreau

66"There certainly is a long history of political conversation,"
thought Joan, as she put down her book on the history
of conversation. In England during the 17th century, coffeehouses had sprung up (before the British switched to tea) where
people joined in conversation with anyone who was sitting
there. The coffeehouses were called penny universities because
you paid your penny and sat down to discuss the current issue
of *The Tatler*. The king even closed down the coffeehouses for
awhile, because he felt they were too subversive (and of course
he was right — any time people discuss ideas it's subversive), but
the people produced such a clamor that they reopened in a week.

Joan wondered how people had handled their political differences, because politics was a hot topic at most of those early
gatherings. She herself didn't enjoy talking politics much these
days. She'd never liked talking with right-wing Republicans.
Not only did she disagree with what they said but they seemed
to idolize Rush Limbaugh and tried to shout her down. But
any differences of opinion seemed touchy lately — so mostly
she and her friends avoided politics and just talked about new
movies and restaurants.

And it wasn't just politics. She had been at a dinner party earlier that week where her husband started talking about organic foods. A couple of the guests were scientists and really lit into Joel, saying that no one really understood science these days, and that all this talk about alternative health had no scientific foundation. Joan tried to switch the topic, but Joel combatively took the opportunity to push the discussion further into alternative thinking, talking about naturopathic healing.

And then she'd had a painful conversation with some neighbors — people she had always felt were good friends with similar politics. Bob and Susan had been going on and on, saying that people who had voted for Gore instead of Nader were just fools. Joan's instinct was to keep quiet about the fact that she had voted for Gore, but she felt she had to admit it if she wanted to avoid feeling like a hypocrite. Every time Joan thought about the conversation, she felt a little sick.

The thing she missed the most was the laughing. She remembered the slumber parties in high school when she and her friends would giggle themselves sick. She supposed that trying on wigs or smearing on makeup had something to do with it, and she could hardly expect to do that with her friends today.

But Joan realized that there had been some good conversations lately. Some of them just silly little things, like the time last week when she and Joel had met an older couple while they were out walking and the couple stopped to admire Joan's little dog. After talking for awhile about how wonderful dogs were they said, "Well, if you ever want us to look after her, be sure to look us up. We only live in Wales."

It was so nice to have friendly little exchanges with strangers. They weren't important conversations, but they somehow lifted your spirits.

They reminded Joan of how most conversations with strangers seemed to involve trying to get something fixed. Some of them were horror stories. One woman had tried to cancel a credit card, yet each month she got a bill with a minimum charge attached. Each month she'd call up the company, who promised to cancel, yet nothing happened. Finally, the woman figured out how to get to the president of the company and get some action. But she'd wasted so much time and energy that she had nothing left for good conversations.

And if it's not some business problem, it's road rage. Last month Joan had watched an older woman trying to parallel park while a young woman in an SUV laid on the horn behind her, yelling at her to hurry up and get out of the way.

So, thought Joan, things aren't looking too good for conversation these days. By the time you get home at night, your interchanges with people have been so unpleasant that you just want to hide. Friends have no time. There are no places to gather. And people seem too rushed and preoccupied to value good conversation. People have too many emails to get through.

Even when she was with people, conversation didn't always flow easily — particularly at big gatherings where she knew few people. It was so hard to think of something to say at these parties. And then when she found someone she was interested in, she felt like she couldn't monopolize their time and should move on. But she couldn't figure out how to do it without seeming awkward and brusque.

Joan thought about the comments of a woman she'd met recently — a woman from Germany who had said, as she held up her latte cup, that the main difference between Germany and America was that when you had a latte in Germany you took a couple of hours to talk with friends, but in the U.S. people drank lattes for fuel, getting their coffee at a drive-through stand and drinking it alone in the car.

It seemed like a good way to characterize the state of American conversation — drinking alone in your car. Maybe with all the new-fangled things people have in their cars — faxes, cell phones, television — people wouldn't notice that they were lonely. Joan wondered if conversation was dying out

because people were working so many hours or if the cause
and effect were reversed — people were working long hours
because everyone had forgotten how to converse.

Joan sighed again, feeling thankful that at least she liked
to read.

Cultural Change

Most of us know what the basics of good conversation are, but
we have to see conversation as a commitment to change the
larger culture, to move from a culture that doesn't seem to care
about conversation to one that does. We need to make conversation so interesting and exciting that people will be lured back
into it and begin to see it as one of the most exciting things
they can do. We need to create a convivial culture. Here are
some ideas for conversation and social change.

Number One: Don't Be Negative

> *There is no better symbol of communal life than the
> banquet.*
> — Martin Buber

> *Do not waste yourself in rejection; do not bark against the
> bad, but chant the beauty of the good.*
> — Ralph Waldo Emerson

I certainly don't like being around a phony niceness, where
the other person is always smiling and never reveals anything
real. I prefer a sharp tongue and cutting social commentary.
I've always liked the quote attributed to Alice Roosevelt
Longworth: "If you can't say something nice about someone,
come sit right here by me!" My husband and I have a magnet
on our refrigerator that says, "You say tomato; I say fuck you!" I
must say that sometimes this just about sums up our relationship, but I get a little worried when people see it and laugh
uproariously, leading me to wonder just what people really
think of us. Perhaps my tongue is sometimes a little *too* sharp!

I think all of us have grown tired of people who are just plain negative all the time. They carp and rail against everything. Now, what they say may very well be true, but they just drive everyone away. One habit is particularly unpleasant — always saying how stupid everyone is. You assume, of course, that they'll find you to be stupid as well, so you become guarded instead of free.

This is particularly important when you are talking about sensitive subjects. For instance, when you disagree with some policy of the government, sometimes it's better to talk about the positive things we could be doing instead. People's hackles tend to go up when they hear negative political statements, or they get so tired of hearing negative things that they just shut them out. Instead of talking about how bad the environment is, talk about some of the neat things you've seen people do that help the environment. Instead of talking about how bad it is to have so many homeless, go on the Internet and find positive stories about things people are doing. If you're against war, talk about how to build peace.

The most common problem I encounter, though (hanging around the academic world, as I do) is having people argue with everything I say. You say something and they find all the exceptions or opposing facts. Good grief! Maybe if they threw in an occasional comment such as, "Well that's an interesting idea. I'd never thought of that before," it would be more palatable. But they seem to get into kind of a habit of disagreeing. I try to steer clear of people like this. No sense wrestling with their negative energy.

So try to think of conversation as a celebration or, as Buber, says, "a banquet." Conversation should be experienced as part of the dance of life, like music. Maybe there's nothing as close to it as jazz players who listen and respond as they play. If you need to learn to become more positive, start having more evenings of fun such as playing board games, having singing evenings, or watching funny movies together. Avoid serious conversations for awhile until you learn to enjoy others.

Number Two: Create I/Thou Conversations

Human life and humanity come into being in genuine meetings.... Again and again the Yes must be spoken.

— Martin Buber

I remember one night long ago sitting in a restaurant with a friend who was telling me about Martin Buber and his ideas of "I/Thou," of Buber's dedication to approach life not as an object to be manipulated or exploited but as a subject to connect with. It was one of those times when I came face to face with an idea that transformed me, changed the way I saw the world, influenced the way I lived my life. Appreciating Martin Buber wasn't a matter of being convinced — it was the age-old experience of a light going on, a sudden conversion. I knew what he said was true and I would spend the rest of my life trying to fully understand.

He said that we have the choice of approaching another person as an *it* or a *thou*. When we approach someone as an *it*, we manipulate and exploit. Even when we're just trying to persuade or convince, we risk treating the person as an *it*. When we approach someone as a *thou*, we see the person as an expression of the eternal thou, the ultimate reality of the universe. That is when we truly encounter connectedness and begin to experience life with exuberance and transcendence.

When you begin to work toward I/thou relationships, you quit trying to pressure other people. When you disagree, you simply see that you have different views of the truth, but that the relationship is more important than being right. You can still learn from each other. This concept becomes even more important when people disagree about big issues of tremendous social consequence such as abortion or welfare. It's hard not to want to tromp on the other person. But if you only try to prove they're wrong, that just hardens your heart as well as hardens their resolve.

I remember once hearing an older woman handle someone's racist comment. We were sitting in a sauna at a local swimming pool and talking among ourselves. One man said something like, "Black people are just lazy. I haven't seen one that wants to work." Even though I was already pretty warm, I felt my temperature go up even further, and I was about to burst out with a denouncement of his racist comments. Thank goodness an older woman spoke up first. She said, "Well, I can understand how you might feel that, but what I've found is that when someone doesn't offer me a job, I tell myself that I don't want to work. It's easier than trying again and again and getting rejected. Have you found that?"

Well, everyone responded to her questions, and as they talked, they began to sound less racist. She treated them with respect, as *thou*, but she also gave her view point, expressing herself as *thou*.

Ever since I observed that woman, I've tried harder to practice the I/thou philosophy that I love so much.

Number Three: See Conversation As the Search for Integrity and a Quest for Kindred Spirits

People have a very acute appreciation of the price they have paid for outward peace and quiet: the permanent humiliation of their human dignity.

— Vaclav Havel

The person who tries to live alone will not succeed as a human being. His heart withers if it does not answer another heart. His mind shrinks away if he hears only the echoes of his own thoughts and finds no other inspiration.

— Pearl S. Buck

How does one educate for courage? Through nourishing trust. How does one nourish trust? Through one's own trustworthiness.

— Martin Buber

Teach the girl it is no part of her life to cater to the prejudices of those around her. Make her independent of

> *public sentiment, by showing her how worthless and rot-*
> *ten a thing it is. It is a settled axiom with me, after much*
> *examination and reflection, that public sentiment is false*
> *on every subject. Yet what a tyrant it is over us all, woman*
> *especially, whose very life is to please, whose highest ambi-*
> *tion is to be approved. But once outrage this tyrant, place*
> *yourself beyond his jurisdiction, taste the joy of free thought*
> *and action, and how powerless is his rule over you.*
>
> — Elizabeth Cady Stanton

One Saturday morning when I was in high school, my mother had given me a ride to school for band practice. It was cold and icy out and some of the boys were driving their cars fast and stomping on the breaks so they'd spin around in the middle of the parking lot. My mother, the only adult watching this spectacle, went to get the band director to put a stop to it. After the boys were scolded, they were upset. One of them said, "Who was that old biddy!"

There I stood. Do I turn away and pretend I hadn't heard or that I didn't know who the woman was?

"That's no old biddy," I said. "That's my mother." And I walked away, fighting back my tears. I was excruciatingly embarrassed, but I've always been happy I said it. At least I felt at peace.

Our ultimate need is for integrity: to know what we believe, to express what we believe, and to act on what we believe. We carry that out through conversation — with our selves, with people of the past, with people around us. But speaking up isn't easy. We need to join with kindred spirits.

When I was little, I read *Anne of Green Gables*. She was always searching for "kindred spirits," and somehow that captured my imagination. I've always been on the lookout for them. Once you find kindred spirits, though, you must tend them. Set up dates for lunch, have potlucks, ice-cream socials — constantly strive to bring these special friends together. You can't guarantee what will happen. Maybe they won't even like

each other. Or maybe you'll be lucky and form a commitment to each other to support each other and listen to each
other — form a Saturday Club like Emerson, Hawthorne, and
Longfellow. Here is where you practice saying what you think
and feel. Here is where you practice listening. Here is where
you feel free to be excited and express your true self.

Earlier I referred to the group formed by Tolkien and C. S.
Lewis called "the Inklings." Lewis wrote about the influence of
the group: "Alone among unsympathetic companions, I hold
certain views and standards timidly, half ashamed to avow them
and half doubtful if they can after all be right. Put back among
my friends and in half an hour — in ten minutes — these same
views and standards become once more indisputable. The opinion of this little circle ... outweighs that of a thousand outsiders
.... It will do this even when my Friends are far away."

In his book, *Collaborative Circles: Friendship Dynamics and
Creative Work* (2001), Michael Farrell, professor of sociology at
the University at Buffalo SUNY, describes many such circles
that creative people have turned to. He quotes Henry James
about the importance of such circles: "The best things come ...
from the talents that are members of a group; every man works
better when he has companions working in the same line, and
yielding to the stimulus of suggestion, comparison, emulation.
Great things have of course been done by solitary workers, but
they have usually been done with double the pains they would
have cost if they had been produced in more genial circumstances." Farrell describes several such circles: the Inklings; the
French Impressionists; the Fugitives, poets that included Robert
Penn Warren and John Crowe Ransom; John Steinbeck's Pacific
Grove circle; the Rye Circle that included Joseph Conrad, Ford
Madox Ford, Stephen Crane, Henry James, and H.G. Wells;
and the Bloomsbury group, with Virginia Woolf, John Maynard
Keynes, E.M. Forster, and Lytton Strachey.

We tend to think that the small group is important only
for social change, and I've always thrilled to Margaret Mead's
words, "Never doubt the ability of a small group of committed

citizens to change the world, indeed it is the only thing that ever has." But even the lonely, individualistic, iconoclastic artists have needed their groups. Integrity is difficult to maintain alone. As Lewis said, when he was around unsympathetic people, he not only would feel ashamed of his views, he would begin to doubt them.

So strive for integrity and make it possible by surrounding yourself with kindred spirits.

Difficult Situations

> *If you ever have to support a flagging conversation,*
> *introduce the topic of eating.*
>
> — Leigh Hunt

> *The techniques of opening conversation are universal.*
> *I knew long ago and rediscovered that the best way to*
> *attract attention, help, and conversation is to be lost. A*
> *man who seeing his mother starving to death on a path*
> *kicks her in the stomach to clear the way, will cheerfully*
> *devote several hours of his time giving wrong directions to*
> *a total stranger who claims to be lost.*
>
> — John Steinbeck

As we try to create a convivial culture and we begin to see conversations as an I/Thou experience of life, we can more easily handle the challenges of conversation — how to meet new people, handle criticism and hostility, and learn to say no. If we remember that conversation is a sacred act, helping create the flow of energy throughout the universe, we'll be able to understand how to approach the difficult situations.

Meeting New People

I think most people I know would agree that I am pretty comfortable in social situations, but I still get that sense of dread when I go to a place where I don't know anyone. Many is the time I've had to keep myself from turning around and going home before I plunge into a crowd of people at a big party. In fact, I've even driven to a house where a party was going on, then had second thoughts and driven back home.

Now, sometimes I end up enjoying myself, but all in all, I don't think much of large social gatherings. I had a friend who just plain turned down invitations to large events. It was a matter of principle, he said. The amount of energy you put into something like that rarely seems worth it — conversation usually just stays on the surface and you keep wishing that you were home watching a good video.

Nonetheless, we all find ourselves at functions like this from time to time, so we may as well prepare ourselves to handle the situation the best we can. The best thing to do is to have some stock questions to pull out. Most of us feel foolish chatting about the weather, but it has its uses. It's *transition* talk, really. Here are some tips:

For a start, introduce yourself to people, shake hands, and ask how they know the hosts or how they're connected to the group putting on the event. Then, you can ask them more about themselves. Most of us hate saying, "What do you do?" because we don't like associating core identity with occupation. Besides, you never know if someone is unemployed and you don't want anyone to feel awkward. I like saying, "Do you live around here?" Everyone knows the answer to that. Once you've made a start, you can go deeper to asking people if they *like* where they live. Then you can ask where they would live if they could live anyplace they wanted to. Or you could ask what place they had lived in had been their favorite. (Remember, people usually like talking about their pasts.)

Or start with "Tell me about yourself. What are you involved in?" Then you can ask whether they enjoy their work (or hobby or education, depending on their reply), if it's an area they want to keep involved in the rest of their lives, or how they came to pick that area of activity or study.

The progression is from asking a very easy factual question, to a "feeling" question, and then to an analytical or philosophical one. These questions take people deeper, yet they are not so personal that people feel that their privacy has been violated.

You can also approach people and start with a statement of your own, because some people don't like questions — they feel they're being put on the spot and interrogated. Talk about the horrible traffic. Trite, yes, but remember that this is *transition* talk and that you communicate a lot more than just words — you can communicate an open, friendly, down-to-earth stance by the way you talk about the traffic. It's all in the way you look at people — smiling, nodding, and laughing all communicate a positive and open attitude on your part.

Try to begin with a positive comment. If the person is wearing something striking, comment on it. If you heard them speak, tell them how much you enjoyed their comments. If you sidle up to a group that's already talking, take an opening and say something like, " I certainly agree with you, " or "I think that's a very important point."

Obviously making eye contact is important. In our culture, the person who never looks at you makes you feel unconnected and distant. I met a man the other day who gave me his card, which indicated that he was a CPA. "Wow," I said, "a CPA! You have a lot more personality than I would expect." Now, my response was just a variation on one I'm sure he'd heard a million times, but he came back with a joke I'm sure he's used often, as well. He said, "Do you know the difference between an introverted CPA and an extroverted CPA? When the introvert talks, he looks at his shoes. When the extrovert talks, he looks at *your* shoes." It was a great beginning, and we went on to discuss other things. There's a reason people use "ice-breakers" to begin a conversation — in conversations there can often be a frigid barrier of stiffness to surmount. You can melt the ice with a little of your own warmth.

Another tactic I often use is to comment on a person's name. For instance, recently a man introduced himself to me as David, pronouncing it *Dah-veed.* I asked him about the pronunciation, and after we had discussed his name for a little while, I launched into a discussion about names, saying that I had once read how much our names influence us. If you give a child a strange name, he or she will often get strange responses from people, and those responses will have an effect — maybe positive and maybe negative. For example, if you name a little girl Myrtle, she will get weird responses, and probably not very pleasant ones. However, if you name your child one of the more perennially popular names like David, people will usually approach the child with positive feelings, which the child will pick up.

I often comment that it's interesting to find out what one's name means, and that often the dictionary will tell you. Then I like to tell people what my name means. "Most names," I say, "mean something sort of exalted, like 'gift of God' or 'daughter of sunlight.' But my name means 'dim-sighted or blind.'" Well, that little story breaks down the tension. I have used this particular discussion about names many times when I meet people. It's kind of a "one size fits all" conversational technique that almost everyone is interested in or can comment on. I find that when I talk in a relaxed, easy manner, laughing at my own jokes, the other people relax and have an easier time responding. The pressure's off because they know I can keep talking.

So be prepared with your own stock responses as well as some stock questions. The point is to give it some thought, to be prepared. You take time to get ready for a party — taking a shower, fixing your hair, picking something to wear. So take time to prepare yourself mentally. Think about how to get over that initial discomfort. Do what the athletes do: envision the whole thing. Imagine yourself going up to someone and introducing yourself; hear yourself responding. I have found that if you actually practice things out loud, the response you want will be much more likely to come out.

But be careful about imagining yourself in negative situations. When I was in graduate school I had one economics professor who scared me to death, and I often imagined myself telling him off. Then, one day at a social event, I found myself face to face with him in the middle of a crowd. With all those people, I couldn't escape, so I said hello. He said, "Well, why don't you ever come to see me? I know you go to see Ed Bridges [another professor]." "Well," I replied, "you're too intimidating." He looked at me and said he guessed he had been a little inaccessible, and then we both managed to break free from the crowd and escape. Initially, this was not a conversation that brought joy to my heart. But now it brings me a good laugh. Maybe that really was the best response to him because in the long run it gave me a good story. But I've learned not to imagine myself saying things I would regret, because I never know what will pop out of my mouth.

Thinking about what you can say or imagining yourself carrying on a spirited conversation will help a lot. Before you go into a gathering, remember social events where you felt good, where you felt witty. Your body will relax and the energy will flow more freely. Also, realizing that almost everyone finds this an uncomfortable experience will help put you at ease — you can concentrate on making others comfortable and you'll forget about your own discomfort.

Another dilemma crops up when you find yourself really enjoying talking with someone but you start feeling that you're taking up too much of their time and you need to move on. How do you do it without cutting them short and seeming abrupt? Usually I find a phony reason like excusing myself to go to the restroom or going in search of something to drink. It feels awkward, but we both know it's something we have to do, so maybe it's the best we can do. Perhaps the best way is to tell the truth (almost always the best way) and say, "Well, I've enjoyed talking to you so much, but my inner party meter tells me that for politeness sake we must move on and mingle with others. I hope we can talk again later."

Remember, though — these techniques are only to help you in the beginning. If you feel committed to conversation because it is important to expanding your sense of life, because it is an important way to grow and learn, you will be motivated to try to find a way to make the conversation work. I remember one evening going to an event of some of my husband's friends. Everyone there was a bicycle fanatic and had no desire to talk with me. I sat and fumed throughout the evening, later getting upset with my husband for taking me to such a dull event. I finally realized, of course, that I had ruined the evening myself because I could have found something to talk about. Many of the women there were nurses, and I am always interested in women's work. I could have asked them a lot of interesting questions. Once you begin to see the world as an interconnected web, you will naturally look for connections and be excited when you find them. If you work to become excited about life, that will communicate itself. If you work at being a caring person, you will draw people. I don't see auras, but I can certainly pick up the non-verbal cues of the people who send out waves of positive feeling.

Dealing with Hostility or Criticism

Another conversational dilemma is how to handle hostility or criticism. Our first response to something negative is to fight back and become defensive. My favorite "learning" incident was when I worked in a juvenile detention hall and we had a superintendent who was incredibly controlling. Every time he walked through an area he found something wrong, and we all cringed when we saw him coming.

One day he called me into his office and told me I was too emotional in my work. "No, I'm not!" I responded. And I burst into tears.

Now, who could really blame me for that? His aggressive behavior was intimidating. We tend to act the way others expect us to act. But now I would handle it much differently. The important thing is to be non-defensive. What I should have said was, "Really? You think so? I'll have to give some thought to that! I suppose I could appear emotional some times, but I don't want to appear cold to the kids." Or, I might have said, "You know, you could be right. It's something I have to work on. I think if I were more calm, the kids would be calmer."

The point is that I suggest in my manner that there is really nothing wrong with being too emotional, at least nothing *seriously* wrong. I am agreeing with what he said, but changing the implications. The problem is that supervisors often act as if it were shameful to make a mistake or to need to improve. We redefine the situation by how we react. We might even thank the supervisor for the information. I might have said, "I think you could be right! I think that's probably valuable feedback. I wonder how I could begin to change that."

I'm famous among my friends for being non-defensive. For many years I was the director of a community college women's center, and I did a lot of speaking in the community. Try as hard as I might to be non-threatening, there was usually some sort of hostile response, so I got a lot of practice and became adept at handling hostility. My friends knew, though, that when someone said something hostile, and I replied with, "Well, that's an interesting point," I was really thinking, "You stupid shit! Only a nitwit would think that." (A long way from seeing it as a sacred conversation.)

Giving Negative, Unpleasant Information

One of the problems is that many people really don't know how to give unpleasant news, so they create a negative situation, inviting a hostile response. The biggest problem is probably in the workplace. A lot of supervisors just go around correcting people's mistakes, and pretty soon people start to dread seeing them coming. Actually, the worst thing a supervisor can do is make people afraid to admit mistakes, because then the employees will cover them up or lie about them and the mistakes can't be corrected.

So if you are a supervisor, give some thought to the way you provide negative feedback. First, don't just dispense it freely. It should be at a designated time — a regular, periodic review. If you're always critical, like the juvenile hall superintendent I just described, you will bring out the worst in your employees. If you expect people to screw up, they usually do. So instead of jumping on every little thing you see, give regular, periodic evaluations as a matter of course.

For instance, at that same juvenile hall, my immediate supervisor, Bill Jackson, was a wonderful boss. He was an African American man, retired military. (I note this because I think that both of those difficult circumstances taught him a lot about working with people.) In the beginning of my job I had weekly evaluations when he would ask me to make a list of things I had done well and things I could improve on. Then he would expand on my list of things I had done well and commiserate with the things I could improve on, often saying, "Oh, you didn't do so bad. But let's take a look at what you might want to do in the future." And then we would brainstorm.

I always came away from those evaluations feeling just great — energized and confident and committed to my work. He was my advocate. He cared about me. Bill Jackson was also a very relaxed man, very easygoing. I'm sure he could get angry if he needed to, but he put me at ease and so I could learn and grow. He has always been my model when I've had people reporting to me. Conversation at work should have the same goal as conversation in ordinary life — to help the other's real self emerge, to create an excitement for life, to draw out the best qualities, not to scare and intimidate. Too many employers are confused about this, even though millions of dollars are spent to teach them to manage differently.

Saying No

One of the reasons the art of conversation is in such a bad state is that we have so much to do. Yes, we're working longer hours, yes we have more stuff to maintain, yes we seem to have a million more choices about the way to spend our time than did our ancestors, but I think it's something more. Over and over, people ask me to help them learn to say no.

At the root of the problem is confused thinking. It's not just that people don't really know *how* to say no, they don't know *when* to say no. So once again, we can't just rely on techniques. When we are clear about when to say no, we'll figure out how to do it. I have found an approach that has helped me: when people ask me to do something, I always stall. I tell them that I'll get back to them after I consult my schedule or my family or whatever. The point is to not answer immediately. You can be enthusiastic about someone's suggestion, but just don't say yes on the spot — it's like impulse buying.

Take some time to reflect. This isn't necessarily a rational process, because I've never found that a careful weighing of pros and cons gives me an answer. I consult how I feel. I imagine that I have said yes and then I check out my stomach. If I feel clenched and slightly ill with a sense of dread, I know I have to say no — no matter how good an opportunity it is. I've learned over the years that if I find myself trying to talk myself into something, I probably shouldn't do it.

Of course, rarely are things clear-cut. The more fuzzy your feelings are, the longer you should take to decide. Talk it over with your friends and family. Often when you talk, you discover emotions you had not known you felt. Talking is a method of self-discovery in itself — it's not like giving a planned speech, it's a method of reflection. So talk with people when you have a decision to make.

Then, if you decide that you need to say no, think through how you'll do it. Different situations call for different methods. Always profusely thank anyone who has asked you to do something. Tell them that the opportunity sounds fascinating and you're very flattered to have been asked, but that you will not be able to do it. And here is the important point: *you don't have to give a detailed reason.* The better you know someone, the more you will want to tell him or her the truth, but in most cases don't elaborate.

Try to remain as close to the truth as you can. I don't think little white lies are necessarily immoral, but you usually get caught. Imagine that someone asks you to come to dinner and you don't want to say that you don't want to come, so you say that your car isn't working and you can't get there. They will probably respond that they would come and pick you up or arrange a ride. Maybe you say that you need to get to sleep early because you have to get up early. They might respond that they plan to have the evening over early. A better thing to say is that it just won't work, but you hope you can come another time. Or, you can say that you already have plans, even if your plans are only to spend the evening at home.

Sometimes people will argue with you. Let's say you've been asked to chair a committee. First you feel flattered, but you remember to tell them you'll get back to them and you start to examine how you feel. You discover that you feel slightly ill whenever you think about it. Even though you know it would be good for your career, you know that if you hate doing it, you probably won't do a very good job, so you call up the person and tell them how honored you feel by their invitation but that you won't be able to accept it. Then they start arguing — "Oh, but you're the absolutely best person for the job." "I don't see how we can carry on without you." "I sure hope things don't fall apart if you decide to disappoint us." "What would we do if everyone said no?" People first try to flatter you, then to make you feel guilty, then to shame you — a clear violation of the principle of I/thou.

The only way to handle this is to refuse to be caught by their devious means and avoid debating each reason they use to pressure you. You don't have to justify yourself to them. The best thing to do is to listen to them and respond, "Well, I appreciate what you are saying, but I won't be able to do it." You simply keep repeating what you said, and then try to cut off the conversation as soon as you can. "Thanks so much for asking me, but I'm afraid I have to go now. I hope there will be other occasions that we can work together. Bye."

If you know the other person well and you want to support their work, one alternative is to tell them you cannot do what they are suggesting, but that you could do something else. It's better to offer them something specific. You can't chair the committee, but you would be glad to be on the committee, for instance.

Saying no, then, can become much easier. If you have a hard time making up your mind, call a friend and talk about it. As you talk, things seem to become clearer. (It's nice if you have a friend you know will encourage you to do what you want. I know that a lot of my friends call me when they're making a decision because I almost always encourage them to say no.)

Handling difficult communication gets better with practice. We usually can't remember all the things we want to remember when we're faced with the situation. I've found it helpful to create a list of "conversation don'ts" that I can reflect on periodically.

Conviviality Blockers

We've talked about most of the ways conversation can build a convivial culture, but there are some bad habits we can get into that we might not be aware of. So here are some last little reminders. It's a list to put on your refrigerator or keep in your pocket and whip out before you go into an event. Ask yourself where you fall on these. Most of these things are just habitual responses that you might not even be aware of, so start paying attention.

Avoid a Crabby Habit of Mind

I've already mentioned this, but try not to slip into a whining, complaining mode. John Gottman, one of the most perceptive researchers on relationships, warns about slipping into a "crabby habit of mind" — scanning your environment for things to complain about. You swear at the driver in front of you; denounce the slowness of the cashier at the grocery store; point out to your spouse that she left the milk out. This hurts your relationships, and ultimately affects your entire health and well-being. We all do it, particularly when we're under stress. Gottman recommends consciously looking for things in your life you can appreciate instead of criticize. Part of our competitive culture is always being on the alert for flaws in your potential competitors. Give it a rest.

Don't Be a Know-It-All

I have an awful habit of doing this — a carryover from years of taking classes and having to appear that I knew something, I guess. For instance, if people are all excited about a new book they've discovered, I don't have to say that I've already read it, even if I have. I can say, "Oh, yeah, I've heard of that book, it sounds really interesting. Thanks for the suggestion."

There's just no need to try to prove you have superior information. Even if you don't agree with someone else, you can stay open. I was reminded of this recently when a friend was telling me about hurting his knee when he was doing something athletic. I asked, "Have you tried arnica gel?" He hadn't heard of it, and I said, "It's a homeopathic remedy." "Oh no," he sneered, "I'd never try that." Well, I don't usually proselytize about using homeopathic remedies, something I've been doing for many years, but using arnica gel is becoming pretty standard for a lot of athletes, and it doesn't mean they're wackos. It hurt my feelings that he would dismiss my suggestion like that. He could have said, "Oh, I haven't ever used it. I'll give it a try!" It doesn't mean he has to follow up, but he would have shown me that the relationship with me was the most important thing.

When you're a know-it-all, you not only risk damaging your relationships, but you also cut yourself off from new information and new ideas.

Don't Argue with Everything the Other Person Says

Some people take exception to everything you say. You might say, "What a beautiful day!" and they'll respond, "Well, it's not as nice as yesterday." If we're trying to make contact with people, it happens more easily when we affirm what they're saying. Most people will feel a burst of energy when you say, "Yes, isn't it beautiful!" When I was young I would have sneered at this seemingly meaningless sort of talk, but this is as much non-verbal as anything — it's a gesture of affirmation to the other person.

Don't Overwhelm the Other Person

Always keep alert regarding how you are affecting the other person. Although I think that most people appreciate enthusiasm, it can overwhelm some people, particularly introverts. If I feel that I'm coming on too strong, I pull back and become more low key. Conversation must be reciprocal, and that means staying alert to what's going on.

Don't Confront People

Several years ago, when people were excited about assertiveness training, I found that people sometimes used their new skills to tell others off. They confront someone and say, "I just want you to know that I find you irritating!" They would do this under the guise of honesty and authenticity.

I would never suggest such a tactic. If you do that sort of thing, pretty soon everyone just wants to run and hide when they see you coming. Once you have attacked people, you will never be trusted again. I was in a committee meeting and we were making a decision, and I said, "Well, so and so tends to take too long when she talks." Another woman said to me, "Well, so do you, Cecile." I was stunned. Later, the other committee members reassured me: "I don't know what Jane thought she was doing. You don't take too long, Cecile."

Whether the woman was right or wrong isn't the point. The point is that I will never trust her. I will try to avoid being around her. Too many times this woman has done something like this. She'll act really nice for awhile, and then one day, when your guard is down, she slips the knife in. I'm not sure she's aware of what she's doing, but anyone who wants to connect with others should do a self inventory on this list of bad conversational habits.

Barriers to Conversation

As we work to rekindle the art of conversation and create a convivial culture, we need to understand the barriers to conversation. It's not enough to change our personal lives or to learn new conversational techniques. There are certain things in the wider society that discourage conversation — institutional barriers that require more than personal change.

No Time

When I ask what the cause of this conversational decline is, people come up with lots of reasons, but the biggest one is no time. We have no time because we work too long. We spend too much time at the malls or in front of the television or sending emails. Here's where we have to move in the direction of Europe and press for shorter work hours.

Nothing to Talk About

But our time famine isn't the only barrier. One woman, in a discussion about conversation, said that the reason we don't have good talks these days is that we have nothing to talk about. She felt that our lives are so dull and uneventful that we have no stories to tell, and without stories, conversations can become just shallow exchanges of pleasantries. I think she may be on to something. Research reveals that we spend the majority of our time away from work shopping or watching television or online, so we're not having real experiences that we can talk about.

And as we increasingly interact with computers, the workplace generates fewer interesting experiences as well. When my daughter was in college and working as a waitress, she always had lots of stories about the customers or other workers. Now that she's a computer programmer, she can't even really explain to me what she does. Since she spends most of her time reacting with a machine, there's no more juicy gossip.

With nothing interesting to talk about, more and more people just talk about money. I've always enjoyed eavesdropping in restaurants, and I used to get so involved with other diners' conversations that I was tempted to ask them to speak up. But for the past few years all I've heard is people talking about their stocks and benefits.

People used to talk about relationships. Women would trade stories and commiserate about husbands or boyfriends. But this subject seems to have been spoiled as well. Since we all want to appear successful and give the impression that our lives are perfect, we don't talk about any relationship problems we might be having. (Actually, as people increasingly use cell phones in public, my eavesdropping experiences have improved. People not only discuss intimate experiences on the cell phone, they always seem to talk louder.)

No Place to Talk

But maybe we no longer talk together because we have nowhere to do it. Ray Oldenburg shows in his book *The Great Good Place* how important it is to have public places to gather, places that are small, intimate, local, and safe — the exact opposite of the ambience of most of our communities. In Paris there's typically a café on every block, in England a pub within walking distance for everyone. But now, as the US leads the industrial world in corporate development, the little guys are forced out. I find it questionable whether the chain coffee shops will be able to fill the role of the small, independent café. I'm really not sure they can create the feeling we need, no matter how many fireplaces they add.

Talking Online

Many people today are asking whether conversation is being undermined by the Internet. Probably the best work has been done by Sherry Turkle with her brilliant title *Alone Together* — a phrase that seems to sum it all up. I've tried many times to not get irritated when my husband and I are on a walk with our dog and my husband takes out his iPhone to answer an email. (I tell myself it doesn't matter because he doesn't talk much anyway.) But I never have the self-control I want, so I've finally asked him to stop. It really does make a difference.

And that's just email. I heard a bizarre story of a teenage boy visiting his dad (divorced from his mother). While working with his dad he cut his leg. While his dad phoned the hospital, the boy took a picture with his smart phone and posted it on his Facebook page. His mother saw it (immediately — which I find bizarre) and texted his father, asking what was happening. Another time the boy hurt his knee skateboarding and posted a picture, which the mother saw and called the father to yell at him — even before the boy was home and the father found out about it.

This is weird to a lot of us. But we can't go around talking about how awful this is because we'll cut ourselves off from younger people for sure. I try to ask questions. When I give workshops I ask young people how they feel about always being plugged in. They don't necessarily like it, but don't know what to do. If you're the only one not wearing earphones, what good will it do?

Turkle talks about the fact that when we talk online we learn to manage our image — you can delete that sentence before you send the email or your tweet. There's less spontaneity. But probably the scariest thing she's worried about is that people will eventually learn to substitute robots for real human contact as she's found some doing. She feels these devices offer companionship without the demands of relationships.

But, again, we can't go around ranting and raving. Just keep having conversations. It's keeping alive an ancient art that people will return to. So I love Turkle's declaration: "I am a partisan for conversation. To make room for it, I see some first, deliberate steps. At home, we can create sacred spaces: the kitchen, the dining room."

I just wish she would have included the living room as well.

The Argument Culture

Too many of us are afraid that if we say what we really think and feel, we'll be attacked or laughed at. I'm not sure I've ever really recovered from the book discussion group I was in when one woman would roll her eyes and look disgusted whenever I said something. (*The Wall Street Journal* had a story once that said that a whole new profession was emerging — therapists for people in book groups. One man interviewed said that the people in his book group were some of the meanest people he'd ever met.)

Linguist Deborah Tannen dubs us the "argument society" and wonders whether we can move to a society of dialogue — a culture in which we listen to each other without attacking each other, in which we learn from each other instead of trying to beat each other down, a society in which discussion is not a form of combat but a form of barn raising.

Maybe our biggest barrier is the conversational skills we've learned from our culture, skills that aren't working. Our schools teach us that talking together is a contest to see who knows the most or who is the smartest. At work we feel that we can't expose our real selves, that we must pretend that we know what we're doing, pretend that we're competent, "together" people. (One of the reasons I quit being an administrator was because I found it boring to act like an administrator.) Our faith groups often make us sit facing front, listening to the anointed one, only repeating the written words before us.

The biggest barrier we need to overcome is the acceptance of the idea that "you're on you're own" and that it's "everyone for himself."

The Convivial Culture

The conversation strategies discussed in this chapter are good for almost any setting, but the focus is to create a living room revolution, having people over to gather and enjoy themselves. I do a lot of this, having discussion groups, movie nights, potlucks, political meetings, and on and on.

What's the key to the success of these gatherings? Informality. Over the years I have discovered that the best hosts are ones who don't worry about anything. For instance, we have some wonderful friends who have extended their hospitality to many, and they are always relaxed. When you come in, they might ask you if you want some tea, but it might be you who makes the tea on your own. Their house is, of course, clean, but it's not obsessively neat. They usually have various projects in process that can't be cleared away. Often we call them and see if they want us to bring dinner over. Or we just take a movie. It's no big deal. No pressure. I want my guests to feel relaxed as well, so my motto is always "It's good enough!"

The one thing I try to do, though, is always have flowers. They make me feel happy and help create conviviality. Maybe flowers are the true symbol of conversation. They grow and they bloom because they're receiving the sun and the rain, a connection with all of life. Maybe this is what we're meant to do in each of our conversations.

Chapter 7

Civil Discourse

*Here is the true meaning and value of compassion and
non-violence when it helps us to see the enemy's point
of view, to hear his questions, to know his assessment of
ourselves. For from his view we may indeed see the basic
weaknesses of our own condition, and if we are mature
we may learn and grow and profit from the wisdom
of the brothers who are called the opposition.*

— Martin Luther King Jr.

On January 8, 2011, Congresswoman Gabby Giffords was shot in the head and critically injured at a supermarket where she was meeting with constituents. It was reported as an assassination attempt.

On April 16, 2012, Rocker Ted Nugent said that he would be "dead or in jail by this time next year" if President Barack Obama was re-elected, comparing Obama and his administration to "coyotes" that needed to be shot, and encouraging voters to "chop [Democrats'] heads off in November."

On February 26, 2012, Trayvon Martin, an innocent Black teenager, was shot and killed on the street.

On March 2012, Rick Santorum, right-wing candidate for the Republican presidential primary, visited a firing range in Louisiana. As the candidate took a few shots at a paper target, a woman shouted, "Pretend it's Obama!"

The New York Times wrote in its editorial on March 7, 2012 that the Republican primary campaign had been "relentlessly nasty, divisive and vapid." The right wing has been saying horrible things. In particular, there was the despicable episode of Rush Limbaugh calling a young law student a slut and a prostitute because she was campaigning to have insurance companies pay for women's contraception. Limbaugh even called for her to post a sex tape of herself on YouTube!

You know about all of these, but how quickly they fade into the past. Psychiatrist Robert Lifton coined a term to explain our response to the nuclear bombs we dropped in Japan at the end of World War II — *psychic numbing*. We had to shut down our emotions because it was just too much for us to handle. It seems like the same thing is happening today. We simply are no longer outraged by all of this incivility. We've accepted it as normal.

I began this book with a description of a relatively minor uncivil behavior in a parking lot, and I asked how we can move from a culture of "every man for himself" to a caring culture concerned about the common good. But as I think about the short list above, I begin to feel that things are hopeless.

There is so much anger and hate out there. We need to ask ourselves what's wrong. Why are we so angry and vituperative? What can we do?

Maybe our declining civility is because things are changing and people are afraid.

Maybe our declining civility is a result of pent-up *racism* exploding over Barack Obama.

Maybe it's an effort to keep connected to our crowd. If they're shouting hate, we feel like we want to join in.

Maybe it's the result of inequality where the social connections are severed and we feel alone and abandoned. Like an injured animal, we strike out at anyone around.

Probably all of those.

But we know, in part, the incivility is growing because people don't understand the importance of a civil public life.

There's a belief system that being an asshole is a good thing. Not long ago I heard some staff at a major university discussing their supervisors. Many of the bosses had just read Steve Jobs's biography and were concluding that if they, too, were assholes, they'd be more likely to get ahead. Imagine!

What we are seeing is a continuing decline of civil discourse. We're just not nice to each other anymore, and although you could dismiss rudeness as being irritating at best, I think it's more profound than that. Earlier I wrote about Solnit's account of the San Francisco earthquake. She tells the story of philosopher Williams James's visit to San Francisco after the earthquake. He was at Stanford teaching. He went up to San Francisco and was astonished by the cheerfulness, the calmness.

James writes that what he saw was something he had long searched for — the moral equivalent of war. He felt that one of the reasons we had wars was because people were essentially bored with their lives and that war awoke something within people that made them feel more alive. He felt that we would always have wars unless we found something that was so emotionally challenging that human beings would turn away from war. He saw this after the earthquake, a situation of response to disaster that he felt would "inflame the civic temper as past history has inflamed the military temper." He saw the "civic temper" as something people yearned for, even if they didn't realize it.

What James is saying is that we *need* to be connected to each other, not just in our families and our neighborhoods, but in public life, the civic life. It's a deep part of human nature, and when it doesn't exist we're unhappy. So, if we are to do something about uncivil discourse, we need to find ways to lure people into being involved in the civic life. When people discover the joy it can bring, they'll begin to treat each other differently.

So let's think this through. What could we do to create a more civil public life? We need to examine both private conversation and public conversation, but it's always best to begin by joining with others to make a change. Making changes together is the essence of civic life. So let's look at that first, and then examine individual conversations.

Better Together

One of my main themes is that we always do better when we come together to work things out. And we could do this to resist the uncivil discourse of public meetings. For instance, Van Jones, former special advisor to the Obama White House, author of *Rebuild the Dream* (2012), says that when the Tea Party disrupted town hall meetings we should have been organized to stand up and chant — maybe something like "Hope, not hate!" He said that we must find ways of speaking up to support Martin Luther King's belief that the "American Dream reminds us that every man is heir to the legacy of worthiness."

But let's expand on Van Jones's idea. Before a meeting, gather with other progressives and create a plan together. For instance, at the beginning of a meeting, the person in charge should address the issue, making it clear that "bullying" won't be accepted. The facilitator could say something like this: "I don't expect anything negative to happen tonight because we have a history of civil discourse in our community. But because of certain national incidents, I've been asked to address the issue. I'm sure you all feel as I do, that attacking people verbally is not acceptable. That we should respect each other and learn from each other. So I'd like to work with you to develop some guidelines for this evening's conversation. Let's begin by turning to the person next to you and coming up with a few guidelines for congenial meetings."

Then, after people have had the opportunity to talk together, have them propose some informal guidelines to the whole group. The crowd will probably come up with ideas similar to the ones we've described as good conversation, because they're common sense. When people feel they have helped develop the guidelines, they will be much more likely to observe them and enforce them. Further, when people talk to each other face to face, they will always treat each other with more respect and caring.

And of course, everyone should have their cell phones ready to take videos and post them immediately to the Web. No one can ever count on being anonymous anymore. Maybe that should also be announced in the beginning.

And finally, maybe we should do what we did in the flash mob I described earlier. Maybe we should be prepared to burst into singing something everyone knows, like "You are my Sunshine" and then organize ourselves into a conga line and dance out into the streets.

Creating congenial political meetings should be a goal of the whole community — just as people are coming together to do something about bullying with kids. We need a national outcry. It should be a campaign. We should have T-shirts, parades, signs, etc. saying "Bring Back Civility!" We should schedule community meetings, write letters to the editor, and post the issue on neighborhood blogs. Get people talking. Above all, bring it up in your conversations with people. Say something like "I've been really wondering what we can do about our increasingly uncivil public life. Have you any thoughts about this lately?"

Talk to national groups like the Coffee Party, Everyday Democracy, and MoveOn. A local campaign is always good, so maybe there are churches in your community that would focus on this. I think the best idea I've ever heard, though, is the Listening Project, where people have gone door to door asking people about their ideas and just listening to them. This was used in the South during the civil rights movement, and as people talked and expressed racist views, these views began to temper as they were listened to. There was no argument, no lecturing. Only listening.

On April 29, 2012, Bill Moyers responded to Representative Allen West's claim that there are "79 or 81 communists" in Congress by showing the famous clip of army counsel Joseph Welch, in 1954, crying out to Senator McCarthy in a televised hearing, "Have you no sense of decency, sir? At long last, have you left no sense of decency?" Most of us have been moved by Welch's words, but what I had never known before was that the gallery burst into applause.

The people responded. That's what it takes. We may not be the ones who speak up, but we can support those who do. And we can support them by talking about our uncivil behavior with friends, families, or community groups. This should become, as sociologist Amitai Etzioni suggests, the subject of a national conversation because, as John Dewey said, "Democracy begins in conversation."

Private Conversation

Coming together and creating a plan is not only more effective in addressing a problem, it's usually more enjoyable. It's participating in the civic life that William James described. But, we often run up against incivility in private conversations when we're on our own. How do we respond then? Many of the ideas for handling that come from the guidelines for good conversation.

What do you do if you find yourself in conversation with someone who spews anger and political lies? Over the years, through my reading and experience and conversation, I've become committed to a certain approach — treating people with dignity.

First, we must *always* speak with respect and caring, no matter how we feel. Always treat others with care. That's our ultimate goal — to create a caring culture. But that doesn't mean you have to engage with an angry person. Sometimes you should just walk away. Perhaps that would be a statement in itself. If someone shouts at you and calls you names, explain that you won't be part of an angry conversation. Refuse to engage.

But when you can, try to reach the other person. First, try to talk about something other than politics — a craft, gardening, or the weather. Get to know another side of the person. You can talk with people in a way that helps them feel valued and respected, and someday, you never know, they might remember meeting you — a liberal person who treated them with respect — and feel more open to progressive ideas.

But what are strategies that might allow us to actually state our views without engaging in conflict?

When you try to talk about political ideas, express your idea, but don't push it. Don't try to convince people. When they disagree, don't argue. Shift the conversation back to them by asking them to tell you more about *their* ideas. Say something like this: "My view on this is..., but I'd be really interested in how you developed your idea." Then try to be sincerely curious. Don't try to trip them up with your questions. Just listen. After a certain point, thank them and either change the subject or leave. Say something like, "Well, thank you, I appreciate your explanation. I'm going to give your ideas some thought." Maybe they will respond in kind by asking you about your ideas, but maybe not. Probably not. I would change the subject or try to escape. (When I've been in these situations there's often a voice in my head from a Monty Python movie saying "Run away! Run away!")

Another other thing that can help is trying to find something you can agree on. For instance, you might say, "I agree that our taxes are not well spent — I don't like all the money that goes to wars. I think it would be better spent on education." Then, if there are areas of agreement, you can try to build on that. Be quick to say "good point" or "I agree" when you can.

You might ask for the other person's thoughts about what the government *should do,* what taxes should be used for. How *should* we pay for education? For firefighters? Should federal money be used for local disasters? Or maybe ask, "Do you feel corporations should pay any taxes? Do corporations have too much influence on our government?" Be careful here, though, because it can become disguised pressure.

It's always better to preface a statement with "I think" or "In my experience" or "I've found that" or "It seems to me." Somehow it softens things. When you announce something as categorically true, people feel pressured. So say, "I think taxes on the military should be cut" or "It seems to me that taxes on the military should be cut." Not "Taxes spent on the military should be cut!" Try not to speak with exclamation marks!!!!

I'm sure you know these techniques. I know these steps aren't easy, and I certainly fail at them often. It seems to me, though, that we must keep advocating respect and dignity — to make a stand for civility.

Talking with the Competitive Left

You can get in trouble even when you're talking with people that you tend to agree with. Sometimes liberals become very competitive and want to be the smartest people in the room. (We've learned that being critical makes us seem smart.) I've seen progressives treat each other badly, seemingly vying for the position of being the most left wing. For instance, I remember a woman saying to me, "You're so naïve, Cecile." (I think I had said something like "Let's give Obama a chance. He's got bigger obstacles than we can even imagine.") I still feel upset about that. I should have replied, "Really! I'm interested in hearing why you say that?" Instead I just stood there.

It's sometimes hard to disagree with people like this because they're often very quick and very well informed. I don't do well with them because I remember very few facts. (I was an English major and we didn't need to know many facts.) But perhaps that doesn't matter because linguist George Lakoff says that we don't change people's minds with facts. And that certainly seems to be true — think of how people on the right deny climate change. Facts don't seem to touch them. Instead, be clear about what you think, but don't try to convince. That makes it sound like you're on the defensive. Go into question mode again.

It's also good to have a story to tell. For instance, I tell people about my time living and working on civil rights in the South in the '60s and how that transformed me, how having a Black president seems phenomenal to me, and how much loyalty I feel for Obama as a result.

I feel strongly that we always need to *try* to be pleasant, which means smiling and laughing when you can. (Again, somehow we've learned that if you don't smile, people will think you're smart.) When you're always ranting about how horrible things are, you lose a lot of people. In particular, I try never to say "Those people are so stupid." Even if we don't say it in front of people on the right, they know we think they're stupid, and it makes them angry. (I think we *do* have a problem with liberal elitism. Many liberals were good students and we learned to have disdain for people not as smart as we are.) Ranting about how stupid people are says that you don't really believe in democracy — government by the people, for the people, and of the people.

Learning from Lakoff

Ultimately we have to give this problem some focused attention. Probably the person who has put the most energy into thinking about civil discourse and effective communication is George Lakoff. I've found his approach to be tremendously helpful. Let's take a look at some of Lakoff's advice.

First, Lakoff suggests that when we think about effective communicators, we should think about Ronald Reagan. Reagan was a successful communicator, Lakoff says, because he talked about values, connected with people, appeared authentic, and made people feel they could trust him. Reagan was successful at this, says Lakoff, because he was an *actor*. Progressives must do this because this is who we truly want to be — people who care about values of fairness and are firmly committed to being caring, authentic, and trustworthy.

Lakoff argues that progressives must talk about liberal *values* instead of focusing on policies. We must talk about the issues of empathy, responsibility, fairness, and justice. (These are values that emerge from at least three of the happiness factors: connection, calling, and control. For instance, justice may be basic to control, because discrimination is an essential lack of control.)

In particular, Lakoff talks about "reframing" — not using conservative terminology. To explain conservative values, Lakoff suggests that values are similar to two different kinds of parents: On one side is the "strict father" who believes that there should be a strong man in charge and that everyone should follow his orders. On the other hand is the vision of the "nurturing parents," who want to raise children with affection and reason.

Within these two belief systems there are certain code words. People on the right talk about "right to life" when they are against abortion. Lakoff recommends never using their words because it just reinforces their views. Instead of "right to life," we try to use the idea of "choice" or women's control over their own bodies.

Above all, it doesn't help to argue. The relationship must be more important than winning the discussion. Lakoff says that progressives must talk about liberal values of fairness, justice, compassion, and equality, and we must help people feel that we, as progressives, are fair, just, and compassionate because of the way we communicate with them.

Those are Lakoff's basic ideas. Now let me go into some more detail.

In the strict-father model, the father is supposed to protect the family from evil, and he must compete to bring home wealth and not be a loser. (When I have discussed this with students, they prefer the word "dominating" or "controlling" father, because even progressive parents often need to be strict.)

The strict-father model believes that kids are born bad and that the strict father must teach them discipline by punishing them so that they will become moral people. They believe that there is an *absolute* right and wrong and that the father knows what is right. (This is similar to our cultural belief in "every man for himself" instead of "we're all in this together.")

Further, if you are moral, you become prosperous. If everyone pursues his or her own profit, it helps everyone. (Shades of the Protestant work ethic. Obviously you are blessed by God if you're making money; if you're not, you're not one of the chosen.)

If some people want government to help, they're called "do gooders" — something that screws things up for the moral people. You *must* pursue your own self-interest.

If you're not disciplined, you can't be prosperous and you are not moral.

So, their argument goes, social programs are immoral because you take away the incentive of people to be disciplined and moral.

For the right, power and morality go together. There is a strict hierarchy: God, humans, nature; men over women; whites over blacks; straights over gays.

For progressives, it's the nurturing-parent model that's relevant. You nurture your children, who will nurture others. Nurture means empathy and responsibility for self and others. This involves protection, fairness, fulfillment, and freedom (correlating to the happiness factors of connection, control, celebration, and calling.)

Progressives want a nurturing, caring leader who is responsible and who is in favor of cooperation, trust, and honesty.

People vote their identity, not issues.

The US population is made up of about 37 percent conservatives, 33 percent progressives, and about 30 percent or so in middle. We must reach those in the middle.

Don't give facts, because that's not what sways opinion.

Don't try to pressure people to agree with you. When we feel pressured, we push back. If we don't feel pressured, we might even pay attention.

Don't argue with conservatives, because then you're in a competitive mode and that's their mode.

Talk with them and ask them what they care about. Don't try to change them or trap them. Try to activate their "nurturing parent," their caring self, which is buried within them. You won't change them then, but you might have an effect in the long run.

Always speak in terms of values, and remember that conservative values are the unfettered free market, individual initiative, pulling yourself up by the bootstraps, and the belief that you can manage your money better than the government can.

They repeat these ideas over and over no matter what the subject is. They make it sound "normal," as if it's common sense. People then come to accept their ideas.

Progressives must learn to talk about values. We must say, "We believe in using the common wealth for the common good so that all of us can be free to pursue our personal goals. Government exists to help people develop their full potential, to empower and protect them as they pursue their potential.

"Nobody makes it on their own: everyone uses the roads that are paid for by taxes; workers are educated in schools paid for by taxes; banks are subsidized by taxes, and we have a responsibility to continue it. People who benefit more from these things should pay more in taxes."

Conservatives believe it's every man for himself, and they're wrong!

So, says Lakoff, we can't let them talk about fear. We must stress hope and joy. Our country is about hope and the pursuit of happiness, about the second chance, and the little person making it.

In fact, says Lakoff, you have a moral obligation to be happy, because then you'll want others to be happy. When you're not happy, you want to bring others down.

Yes, we must also have moral outrage, but we can't express it by attack or denunciation.

We must be grateful for the things we have and enjoy them. If we don't enjoy them, we won't care enough to try to bring them into the future (celebration).

We must talk in terms of hope and think positively. We must counteract fear. If we give into fear, we're giving into the conservatives (control).

We must always present ourselves as moral people (calling).

We must not have the view that we are better than they are: we believe in equality (connection).

Conservatives want to get rid of government, but the country is actually governed by corporations, which are not accountable to anyone.

So there's Lakoff in a nutshell — with my happiness factors inserted. I agree with what he has to say. Lakoff's essential message is that we bring about progressive change by evoking empathy. We need to call forth that essential human quality that cares about others. The most basic way to do this is by connecting with them through caring conversation, whether in "stop and chats" or study circles — experiences that help people care about each other.

It's not easy to keep all of these ideas in mind, so the best thing you can do is form a study circle, which we'll talk about soon. Get together with others and study Lakoff's ideas. Practice trying them out. Each group member should keep a small notebook and record observations throughout the week. Then, during the weekly meeting, participants tell their stories and brainstorm about effective responses. For instance in our Transition group, we have formed a small group we call Community, Calling, and Conversation. We come together to talk about how we are able to talk to people about our ideas without engaging in rancor or anger. In a MoveOn group I also formed, we gathered each week to specifically talk about political discourse — about how we explained our political views that week. We brainstormed and helped each other develop new ways of responding.

Money Values and Public Discourse

Part of our challenge is to understand why we have such ugly public discourse. As we've found before, many of our problems are linked to our values around money. If wealth is our highest value, can we even care about how we talk to other people? If wealth is our highest value, do we care about kindness and honesty and civil discourse?

What Money Can't Buy: The Moral Limits of Markets (2012), by Harvard's Michael J. Sandel, says that we must start talking about our values around money. Sandel calls for public discussion. In a Huffington Post article on April 20, 2012, he says that "market triumphalism has coincided with a time when public discourse has been largely empty of moral and spiritual substance. Our only hope of keeping markets in their place is to deliberate openly and publicly about the meaning of the goods and social practices we prize."

His is an incredible book, going to the heart of many of our problems. Sandel talks about the "skyboxification" of our society, with people in sports stadiums separated according to the price of their seats. The problem, he says, is that wealth stratification means that people no longer mingle. If you don't mingle with people, you won't talk with them. You'll just feel uncomfortable around them. He thinks it used to be a civic event when people went to a ball game, where you met people from all walks of life. Certainly that was always my image of baseball games. I remember how, in junior high, they brought all the kids into the gym to watch the World Series. We were experiencing something together that I can now see was civic life.

Sandel goes on to say, "Democracy does not require perfect equality, but it does require that citizens share in a common life.... For this is how we learn to negotiate and abide our differences, and how we come to care for the common good."

Essentially, Sandel argues that letting market values into every aspect of life diminishes our traditional values of family life, fairness, equality, and democracy and causes us to become cynical and to believe, as I stated in the beginning, that human nature is essentially selfish and that there's no hope.

He reminds us of the things money can now buy — things it couldn't in the past.

For instance, corporations now purchase naming rights. I remember how shocked I was when university buildings began to be named after corporations. I remember giving a workshop in a university classroom where not only did the building have a corporate name, so did the room. Apparently when Bank One purchased the naming rights for the Arizona Diamondbacks stadium, sports announcers had to call the home runs a "Bank One Blast."

Why didn't we rise up when we first saw these naming rights and say it wasn't acceptable? I remember shaking my head and feeling outraged, but I did nothing. And that's Sandel's point. It's gradually slipped up on us and we've done nothing until our whole way of thinking has been changed. Money dominates almost everything.

Maybe we didn't rise up because our sensibilities had been dulled by egregious commercialization. In 2000, a Russian rocket shot into outer space with a giant Pizza Hut logo. Eggs in grocery stores are stamped with ads — the individual eggs, not the cartons. There are commercial messages in public bathrooms and in books. Sandel reports that in 2001, British novelist Fay Weldon wrote a book that had been commissioned by an Italian jewelry company. Weldon was paid to mention their jewelry in the book. In Britain police cars have ads on them. They tried that in this country, but at the time of the publication of Sandel's book, the attempt had failed due to public outcry. See — public outcry can work!

Some of Sandel's examples are seemingly small things. For instance, you can purchase your way out of waiting in line at amusement parks; they're starting to let solo drivers pay to drive in express lanes; kids are paid for reading books. But some things are more significant: Companies are allowed to purchase life insurance policies on their employees, benefitting when they die. And this is even spreading — with strangers buying policies on people as a form of investment. And of course in the past there were no for-profit hospitals or for-profit prisons.

How have we accepted all of this? The more money can buy, the more it matters, and the more we sacrifice other values like honesty and kindness.

Certain things are sacred. We don't let people sell their children, but couples are paying for surrogate pregnancies. Is that a slippery slope? Theoretically we don't let politicians sell their votes, or do we? Isn't that what's happening with campaign money in politics? Aren't politicians selling themselves to the highest bidder? If everything can be bought and sold, is it a surprise that we've commodified everything? And we don't even notice.

Sandel calls for public discourse around our economic values, and I think people are ready for such a discussion. The Occupy movement helped bring it to the forefront, and it's finally an issue we're talking about. I've seen a definite change over the past several years. At one time, when I'd bring up the topic of wealth inequality, people would seem embarrassed. Now they respond. We must continue to work to discuss the issue in a civil manner.

Lessons from History

We're not just talking about stopping uncivil discourse, but creating *civil* discourse! How can we do that? We can learn from history.

We have to remember that the great movements of US history grew because people talked to each other. The spoken word makes a difference. How do you think people learned of the Montgomery bus boycott that was inspired by Rosa Parks's refusal to move from her seat on the bus? People passed the word around themselves.

The '60s revolutions were ignited by students' free-speech demands, their insistence on their right to speak out and be listened to. An explosion of energy was released on December 3, 1964, when Berkeley students were told they could not pass out leaflets about the civil rights movement, and Mario Savio leaped on top of a police car and ignited people with his stirring words, now preserved in a YouTube video:

> We're human beings! ... There's a time when the operation of the machine becomes so odious — makes you so sick at heart — that you can't take part. You can't even passively take part. And you've

got to put your bodies upon the gears and upon the wheels, upon the levers, upon all the apparatus, and you've got to make it stop. And you've got to indicate to the people who run it, to the people who own it, that unless you're free, the machine will be prevented from working at all.

Both before and after those moving words, the students were standing around talking together.

Women in the 19th century talked among themselves as they mended and quilted, but they also gathered with people like Margaret Fuller, who held formal "conversations" to educate and inspire women about the rights of women as well as men. In fact, the 19th-century women's movement was sparked when Elizabeth Cady Stanton had a conversation with Lucretia Mott over dinner. Stanton recounts in her *History of Women's Suffrage*,

> In spite of constant gentle nudgings by my husband under the table, and frowns from Mr. Birney opposite, the tantalizing tone of the conversation was too much for me to maintain silence .... When I first heard from the lips of Lucretia Mott that I had the same right to think for myself that Luther, Calvin, and John Knox had, and the same right to be guided by my convictions, and would no doubt live a higher, happier life than if guided by theirs, I felt at once a newborn sense of dignity and freedom; it was like suddenly coming into the rays of the noon-day sun after wandering with a rushlight in the caves of the earth .... I accepted her words of wisdom with the same confiding satisfaction that did the faithful Crito those of his beloved Socrates.

In the 1960s, feminists were inspired by Black people in the civil rights movement who had gathered together in Freedom

Schools and taught themselves to read and to express their demands and reminded each other through their daily talk that they were human beings too.

The 20th-century women's movement was fueled by consciousness-raising groups, where women gathered in church basements and tiny cramped apartments and talked with each other and told the truth about their lives.

And of course, it's not just US history — but the rest of the world. Everything started with Socrates. He conversed with people as he searched for truth. In his mind, there was nothing more important than talking with people. And he inspired people throughout history and throughout the world.

In Greece, men (unfortunately no women or slaves were involved) gathered in the Athenaeum and worked out the ideas that we now hold to be self-evident — that all men and women are created equal and endowed by their creator with certain inalienable rights, among which are life, liberty, and the pursuit of happiness.

People in the French salons talked about the "rights of man" and helped bring about a revolution that still influences us today.

Across the channel in England, men gathered in coffeehouses to read the newspapers and talk of revolution and democracy.

The list goes on. Throughout history, conversation has enlivened and enlightened people to do great things, to act on the possibilities inherent in being human. This is civil discourse.

And so, through conversation we continue to expand our sense of what is possible in life, to expand the ideas of freedom and liberty for all. The important ideas emerge from people talking together. They don't just happen in the public forum. First people must gather in small groups and hesitantly talk about their dreams for life.

And finally, we can't forget Margaret Mead's words: "Never doubt the ability of a small group of concerned citizens to change the world; indeed it is the only thing that ever has."

Chapter 8

People's Education — Learning for Life

Education is not the filling of a bucket,
but the lighting of a fire.

— Yeats

There is much fine talk in schools about Teaching
Democratic Values. What the children really learn is
Practical Slavery. How to suck up to the boss. How to keep
out of trouble, and get other people in trouble .... Set into
mean-spirited competition against other children, he learns
that every man is the natural enemy of every other man.

— John Holt

At the core of this ... system of education is the belief that
self-knowledge is the only basis of true knowledge.

— John Taylor Gatto

Education by the People, for the People, and of the People

As we observed earlier, on December 1, 1955, Rosa Parks refused to move to the back of the bus, and thus changed American history. On February 26, 2012, Trayvon Martin, a 17-year-old African American was killed, and on March 23 President Barack Obama said, "I think all of us have to do some soul searching to figure out how does something like this happen."

How are these incidents related?

Each provoked a national response, a national conversation. We realized that something was wrong and that we needed to come together to talk. To reflect. To "soul search," as Obama said. Our usual response, when faced with problems, is to expect the schools to fix things. But our educational system, from kindergarten through graduate school, reflects the values of mainstream culture without teaching the art of reasoning and reflection. Our schools perpetuate conventional culture and allow us to be manipulated by forces of society such as television, commercialism, politics, or religion.

If we want change, we need a different kind of education than we get in schools — one that helps us learn to look within and find our own answers. As Gandhi said, "Truth resides in every human heart, and one has to search for it there, and to be guided by truth as one sees it."

Can we help people develop the habit of reflecting on their behaviors and decisions, questioning the status quo, and consciously choosing their actions? This is what education should do: teach people to think for themselves, to recognize attempts to manipulate them, to create new ways of doing things. Our education system fails us, reflecting the society's ills of cutthroat competition and failing to teach people to act on our values of democracy and caring.

But all is not lost. Enter people's education: education by the people, for the people, and of the people. It's a way to bring people together to think and talk together and then act together. Throughout history people's education has been a force for social change. Some teachers do this in their classrooms. We can all do it in our living rooms.

Let's look at one of the most significant examples to embody this approach — Highlander.

Highlander Folk School

Consider Rosa Parks's history-changing action on the bus. Most people think this was a totally spontaneous act of a woman who just got fed up and couldn't take it any more. In truth, Rosa Parks was active in the local NAACP, where they had long talked about such an action. Why did it finally happen? Parks said it was a place called Highlander Folk School that prepared her. Highlander is the hidden secret of the civil rights movement and an inspiring example of people's education.

Highlander took (and still takes) the ideas of conversation and education to their highest level — conscious social change. Over the years Highlander was active in many campaigns for social justice. Beginning in 1932, it worked with unions; it later became a force in the civil rights movement, working with people like Martin Luther King, Eleanor Roosevelt, and Pete Seeger. The song that moved so many of us, "We Shall Overcome," was first popularized at Highlander.

Highlander also started the Freedom Schools that helped some 100,000 African Americans learn to read and write so that they could vote. In those early days of civil rights, Black people were barred from voting by the literacy requirements of most southern states. Black people were required to be able to read a section of the state constitution or some such thing, and of course they were barely given any education.

So local leaders from Johns Island, a little island off Charleston, South Carolina, came to Highlander and said they wanted some teachers to come and teach them how to read. They wanted someone highly educated, someone trained to be a teacher. But Highlander knew that wasn't the answer. They needed someone who believed in the people.

The first citizenship training school was set up on Johns Island, South Carolina, in 1957, and the teacher, Bernice Robinson, was a local beautician with only a high school diploma. She protested that she didn't know how to teach, but Highlander said she was the right person. She certainly proved it when she met with students the first night and started her class by saying to them, "I am not a teacher — we will learn together." She taught them to read with one basic text: the

Universal Declaration of Human Rights which says in Article 1 "All human beings are born free and equal in dignity and rights. They are endowed with reason and conscience and should act towards one another in a spirit of brotherhood."

Citizenship schools spread across the South, teaching Black people to read — but more importantly, restoring to them their dignity and faith in themselves, and affirming their right to be free and equal. And, further, affirming their brotherhood. Dignity, brotherhood, and justice for all has always been the goal of Highlander.

Myles Horton

Highlander was founded by a man named Myles Horton, who is now a hero to people who have looked for ways to educate for social change. He was born in 1905 in the Appalachian mountains and searched for a way to alleviate the poverty of his people in the towns and hollers around him. Attending Union Theological Seminary, Horton was influenced by theologian Reinhold Niebuhr, a passionate advocate of the social gospel — the idea that Christianity meant working for social change to help the poor and the powerless. Later, at the University of Chicago, someone told Horton to visit Denmark and look at the folk schools. He did, and he was transformed.

On Christmas night, 1931, Horton wrote in his journal, "I can't sleep, but there are dreams. What you must do is go back, get a simple place, move in and you are there.... You can go to school all your life, you'll never figure it out because you are trying to get an answer that can only come from the people in the life situation." As Horton later explained, "Highlander programs are designed to help the disadvantaged of all races help themselves, to challenge the status quo in the name of democracy and brotherhood." Highlander's approach? Bring people together to talk and they will find the answers. The wisdom is in the people. Help them build support for each other and people will act.

Why am I telling you so much about Highlander? First of all, it made a huge difference in the civil rights movement. It's legendary in its approach to social change. It holds answers to so many of our questions as we work for a caring, collaborative culture. And second, it changed my life. During the '60s I worked with a Quaker organization, the American Friends Service Committee, in a two-year program bringing white northerners south to work with the poor in Black communities. As part of our orientation, they took us to institutions contributing to social change in the South, and introduced us to Highlander. After we visited Highlander, I saw everything differently. I had always planned to be a teacher, but I had in mind the kind that stood up in front of the class, lectured, and gave out grades. But here, what did they do? They brought people together to talk. For Myles Horton and Highlander, the wisdom was in the people.

Heritage of People's Education

People's education has sprung up wherever injustice exists.

Highlander started out as a *folk* school — a concept which Horton studied in Denmark where folk schools had helped transform a beaten down peasantry in the 19th century.

In the late 19th century, Sweden used the "study circle" (discussed in detail in Chapter 9) to help create a country that is admired by progressives around the world. In fact, Sweden has been referred to as a "study circle democracy," because study circles are still used and seen as vital to the health of their democracy.

In Latin America a man named Paulo Freire became well known for his book *Pedagogy of the Oppressed*, which was based on his literacy work for poor peasants in Brazil. His idea of education was to turn away from the "banking method" — filling people with facts — to the "midwife method" — helping people give birth to their own ideas. Freire was exiled because he insisted that educating oppressed people involved more than just teaching them to read. It meant helping them liberate themselves by learning from each other and taking action.

In Scandinavia, the concept was called "folk" education; in Latin America it was "popular" education. Some in the United

States have called it people's education — education by the people, for the people, and of the people. The approach is the same. The wisdom is in the people. Help people talk with each other in a way that respects both the self and the other, and change will emerge. Help people reflect on their experience, make conscious choices, and take action, and they will break free from the forces that oppress them. Bring people together to talk, think, and take action, and they will find the answers to their problems. We can't depend on experts. We can't depend on the people in charge. We have to do it ourselves, and often it will start in our living rooms as we talk with each other about our problems.

In fact, if you had ever been a fly on the wall at Highlander, you would have thought you were in a living room. It has lots of rocking chairs. The rocking chair strikes the right chord, because it creates a comfortable, relaxed, safe atmosphere, both literally and figuratively. It expresses the atmosphere at Highlander — a safe place to talk because everyone receives respect.

The year 2012 marked the 80th anniversary of Highlander. You can go to the Web archives of PBS to view a Bill Moyers interview with Horton. There is also a new edition of a film produced in 1985. It's called *You Got to Move*, and it tells the story of Highlander. The director, Lucy Massie Phenix, has this to say:

> What is it that makes people stop feeling power-less, and makes them want to change?... It was the process of the people in the film beginning to trust what their own experiences taught them, and their growing refusal to take the judgments of "experts" on matters in their own lives, that shaped the form and meaning of the film, and which makes it universally relevant in a time when this process is taking place all over the world.

Highlander's way of bringing ordinary people together so they can learn from each other is transformative. Ever since my visit there I've tried to find ways to use their ideas in my work as an educator. For many years I was a community college administrator, starting programs with this approach, in particular in the women's movement and the simplicity movement. Now I work in the community and start circles on the movements of happiness and sharing.

I want people to realize that all through history some form of people's education has emerged in times of change: the salons in the French Revolution, the study circles in Sweden, folk education in Denmark, and Paulo Friere's popular education in Latin America. And of course the consciousness-raising groups of the modern women's movement (another experience that changed my life).

It's clear that in this country we can't call it *folk* education or *popular* education — in our culture these don't communicate what we're talking about. Though I like *people's* education, I also use "community education," depending on the circumstances.

Lately, though, thinking about President Obama's comments on Trayvon Martin, the Black teenager who was killed, I'm convinced that we should talk more about *soul searching*. We've got to figure out how to strengthen the values that the Universal Declaration of Human Rights talks about: *freedom, equality, dignity, reason, conscience, rights, and brotherhood.* Community education is about soul searching — asking ourselves where we're going, talking about the fate of people and the planet, talking about how can we move from a violent angry culture where a young Black man can be killed so casually to one where people care about each other. This is soul searching.

We all need to find a way to become engaged in community education. It's vital if we're to create a more caring, collaborative culture. Of course, it also fosters happiness: it brings *connection* as people come together; it helps you find your *calling* as you talk about your values; it brings *celebration* as you laugh together; and it brings *control* as you work together to bring about change.

Community education costs nothing; anyone can do it; and it brings people fulfillment and happiness. A perfect recipe for change.

Features of Community Education

There are three essential features of community education: thinking, talking, and taking action.

Thinking

It strikes many of us that Americans seem to be getting further and further out of touch with common sense. Out of touch with reason — particularly in denying climate change. How the rest of the world must feel, I can't imagine. How did we come to have a society in which people believe lies told to them by Fox News, a society in which people worship celebrities and accept extreme wealth gaps?

We need to take a stand and ask this country to start a movement to do some soul searching, to stop and think. We need to bring people together to think things over. We're overwhelmed by information, ideas, and commercials attempting to influence us. When we're on autopilot and fail to *think*, the "powers that be" are in control. Thinking means that we *consciously choose*, and don't just go along mindlessly. We look at what people in power are saying and then we reflect on our own experience and ask ourselves how the two mesh. We learn to trust our own ability to reason.

Earlier I mentioned the book *The Better Angels of Our Nature*, a work that argues that violence has declined. Author Steven Pinker suggests that one of the reasons is that in the Enlightenment, people learned to reason. They broke free from the religious stranglehold, and as literacy spread, people learned to reason for themselves and began to break free from the oppression of the church and the kings.

I would argue that unless we revive this skill of reason — of thinking and reasoning — violence will begin to increase in our time. Certainly it seems as if this is happening in the

United States. We've seen violent acts that are related to the vitriol and the rancor of the right wing, which promulgates ideas directly in conflict with reason and good science — such as evolution and climate change.

I know that people don't necessarily vote based on reason, but it seems to me that it's not a bad goal to aim for. But it must be "authentic" reason, reasoning that doesn't just parrot the mainstream clichés. My comments above sound as though I'm just denouncing people who watch Fox News. But those of us on the left are not necessarily always good thinkers either. We're too easily influenced by ideas that are promulgated by the educated elite.

One of my favorite stories comes from one of my professors at Stanford, David Tyack, who was the acknowledged national expert on the history of American education. He told us about once sending an article to an academic journal that gave it a "blind" review — the author's name wasn't visible to the reviewer. In this paper Tyack was developing a new idea — one that countered some of his older ideas. The reviewer, not knowing who the author was, became quite indignant, rejecting the paper and telling the author of the paper to study the ideas of David Tyack. Tyack laughed when he told us about this, but he wanted us to see how easily academics come under the sway of being "politically correct" in the form of complying with the ideas of the currently anointed.

So few of us are really good thinkers. We don't have time. We don't have a place. Thinking isn't valued. Creative ideas might make you look foolish. Thinking can make you question your life or turn you into an activist, and that can be scary.

But it seems imperative to encourage our nation to do some thinking and soul searching. We must create opportunities for people to come together and reason together and think for themselves. That's what good conversation is — people thinking things through together, not just turning to the experts.

We must learn to *think consciously* about the consequences of our behaviors. What does it mean to consume so egregiously?

In what ways am I changing the climate? What really makes people happy? We must inspire people to engage in discernment and reflection and a search for the truth.

LEARNING FROM PERSONAL EXPERIENCE

The most unique thing about people's education is the belief that *examining our own experience* will help us find the truth. In school we learn that truth lies in books or in the minds of the experts. Learning from personal experience means reviewing the ideas you've read or heard and asking yourself, Does this ring true to my experience? Is what they're saying congruent with my life experience? It means paying attention to what makes you angry, what makes you sad, what makes you joyful, and asking *why*. It's responding to a feeling, an insight, an instinct, and asking about the meaning. You might get ideas from books, but ultimately you find truth in your own experience. As psychologist Rollo May said, "If you do not listen to your own being you will have betrayed yourself. Also, you have betrayed our community in failing to make your contribution to the whole."

In short, it means learning to listen to your inner voice. That still small voice that's usually drowned out by the noise around us. It's part feeling, part logic; it's part physical, part cerebral. People's education nurtures the individual's inner voice by encouraging them to pay attention. You do it by yourself when you sit and reflect, but most of all, you need do it by talking with other people.

This is the heart of people's education — looking within, talking with others, taking action, and reflecting some more. It's not just for personal change; it's at the heart of social change.

Talking

The best thinking comes from talking together. Of course, we've always said that two heads are better than one. (And obviously this assumes that they are talking!) But books like *The Wisdom of Crowds: Why the Many Are Smarter Than the Few and How Collective Wisdom Shapes Business, Economies, Societies, and Nations* (2004) by James Surowiecki give example after example of people coming together and producing creative solutions to problems.

Democracy needs it; we need it. Self worth comes from saying what we think to others and being true to what we know. Somehow, when we talk together we discover our own truths and learn to express ourselves with confidence. It's hard to speak up in our contentious society, where people argue at the drop of a hat, but when we remain silent, we lose our ability to think as well as our self-respect and dignity.

And because talking is one of the basic human pleasures — one of the essential ways that people connect with each other — there is an intrinsic attraction. Let's show people how much pleasure there is when we come together to talk about what's important and what matters. How delightful it is to gather around the living room to talk — a glass of wine in hand, low music playing, a gas fire in the background. Pure heaven!

Taking Action

Taking action completes the trilogy. Only when we act on something do we really know it. Only by acting do we bring about change. Only by acting do we test our ideas. Only by acting do we build self-respect. We need to take actions, both public and private, that make a difference: we need to change our lives and change our laws. Every day we must act, think about our action and learn from it, then act again.

And we must do it together. The wisdom is in the people.

It's clear that we need to find a way to think, talk, and take action together. We can do this with the exciting approach of people's education, community education, asking this question: How can we use this time honored technique for today's problems? How can we use this transformative approach to create a collaborative culture that cares for the common good. This is not learning that gives you certificates and degrees: It's more important — *it's learning for life.* We can bring people together to think, talk, and take action.

Basic Strategies of Community Education

It's clear that community education isn't about lecturing, tests, and grades, our usual experience of education — an experience that is itself almost as competitive and cutthroat as our whole society. (Who can forget about the stories that circulated a while back about the lengths parents will go to in order to enroll their children in prestigious kindergartens?) How can we make thinking, talking, and taking action come alive?

Many years ago, the growth of folk education in Denmark occurred when that country was economically and psychologically depressed. Folk education founder N.F.S. Grundtvig felt that education should not only *enlighten* but also *enliven.* People not only needed to think differently, they needed to feel differently. They needed hope and dignity and enthusiasm about life. They couldn't just sit and listen, they needed to learn to tell stories, ask questions, listen, respond, and laugh.

Here are the basic strategies we use in community education. As you'll see, they are the same strategies that are involved in good conversation. That's what community education really is — good conversation with a purpose.

Telling Stories

To find ways to inspire people and expand their sense of what is possible, we tell stories. You can tell stories about other people, people who have engaged in courageous and caring activities. When you read a moving story in the newspaper, tell people about it. For instance, I saw a story about a woman who found a homeless teenager sleeping in her yard in the freezing cold of winter. She took him into her house to care for him. That was the beginning of her mission, which she carried out for the next 20 years until she died. She took in dozens of kids and helped them get off drugs and away from the street. She helped them get jobs, earn high school diplomas and go to college. A story like that can make us pause the next time we see a homeless teenager panhandling. Or, for the person who wants to go further, there's the story of a businessman who was mugged by a teenager. Instead of becoming bitter about kids, he created a foundation to train young people to be entrepreneurs. By telling that story, I not only communicate my values, I inspire myself and others to take action.

Telling these stories gives people ideas about what they might do for their calling. But rarely do we read these stories in the newspaper, so we come to believe that no one is doing anything and that nothing can be done. When we hear only stories about our massive problems, we give up in despair. When we hear positive stories, we begin to see life differently. Publications like YES! Magazine have made it their goal to focus on these kinds of stories — stories of vision that give us hope. So seek these stories out (lots of websites available).

But telling our own stories may be the most effective thing we can do. We not only tell people how we feel about environmental problems, we tell them what we're doing to change things. We can talk about how we're composting while we garden, how we eat organic foods so that the soil won't be damaged further, how we keep our thermostat at 65 degrees to save on energy. You don't have to tell people that they must do those things, you just tell them your story. Sooner or later they will think about it. I remember the time I got very sick and conventional medicine was not helping. I recalled a friend at work telling me about her experience with alternative medicine. At the time I had dismissed her as rather flaky, but that conversation ended up changing my life. Not only did I use alternative approaches to get well then, I've been involved in alternative health practices ever since. And now I tell my story to people, and sooner or later many come back to ask me about it.

The most basic thing of all, of course, is giving people the chance to tell their own stories. This is at the heart of community education. People are enlivened when they tell their stories because they discover their own truths within and they discover that they can trust themselves.

Asking Questions

In community education you ask questions. You not only ask people what they're doing, you ask them how they're feeling. When someone tells you about a new job, you ask if the work is satisfying, if the co-workers are good to work with, if the work is exciting. You don't just sit there and try to think of something clever to say. You inquire.

The key is to ask true questions, not questions you already know the answers to. We don't have to be Socrates, but we can appreciate Socrates' example of asking questions to take a conversation to a deeper level. Most of us have heard of the Socratic method, and we don't always think of it in a kindly fashion because it is so often misused — particularly in school, where teachers already know the answers to questions they ask. I remember once when I was speaking to a group of high school kids and I asked one of those teacherly questions like, "What were the causes of the Civil War?" One of the kids groaned and said, "I hate the Socratic method."

I laughed because I realized he was right. Socrates would never have asked a fact-check question like that, one where the real aim is to guess the correct answer or figure out what the teacher wants to hear. Unfortunately, those are the kinds of questions usually found in schools. Teachers are not asking meaningful questions and waiting to see what the answer will be; they're drilling students to respond like computers, because teachers are forced to teach to the test. We need to ask real questions, such as, How can I create community? How can I find my calling? How can I strengthen our democracy?

Listening and Responding

And, of course, you listen. Quietly and intently. Nodding your head, murmuring "Yes, I know!" or "That sounds horrible!" or "I understand." We have a lot to learn from the call-and-response,

"Amen brother!" style of African American churches. Those congregations know that you've got to respond if you want to keep a connection going.

Author Brenda Ueland, in her essay "The Art of Listening" (*Strength to Your Sword Arm*, 1996) offered inspiring words about listening. She said,

> Listening is a magnetic and strange thing, a creative force.... When we are listened to, it creates us, makes us unfold and expand. Ideas actually begin to grow within us and come to life.... When we listen to people there is an alternating current, and this recharges us so that we never get tired of each other ... and it is this little creative fountain inside us that begins to spring and cast up new thoughts and unexpected laughter and wisdom.... Well, it is when people really listen to us, with quiet fascinated attention, that the little fountain begins to work again, to accelerate in the most surprising way.

Laughing

The last element is laughing — the ingredient that adds spice to the conversation, the factor that transforms a dull conversation into a joyful one. When you laugh, you feel transported and free and expanded. You fall in love with life. You are enlivened. People returning from visits to other countries tell me they are astounded at how much more laughter there is in other cultures. When they return home, the people they see on the streets look grim and angry.

We don't have to tell jokes. My best laughs come when I tell others things I would rather they not know — times when I've made a fool of myself. For instance, I tell about the time I worried about making a good impression on my first trip to New York. As I was imagining myself wearing something sophisticated, I tripped over a curb and fell flat on my face. I had to go to New York with a scab on my nose. Or I tell about the time I wore a green dress to a formal wedding (where all the women wore black). When you tell these stories, people feel more connected to you because everyone has had the same kind of thing happen to them. Everyone has tried to keep up an image, only to be tripped up by fate. Whenever I use such stories in my talks, people come up afterward and thank me. Suddenly they don't feel so alone and foolish. They understand that we are all basically alike. Ultimately, the best laughter comes from times when people are just feeling the joy of being together.

Telling stories, asking questions, listening, responding, and laughing. These seem like such basic points about education.

These are the basic strategies that we should use in any setting when we bring people together. Any gathering of people is an opportunity for people's education — whether it's a class, a workshop, a seminar, a meeting, or even a party or social gathering. Any time we come together we must tell stories, ask questions, listen, respond, and laugh. Whenever people gather together we need to inspire them to think, talk, and take action. We can do this in our efforts to create community, to build the sharing movement, Transition, and Occupy. In the next chapter, we'll explore what is to me the most exciting strategy of all — the study circle.

UnLearning

A lot of community education involves unlearning what we've learned in the school system, things that undermine our faith in our own ability to think for ourselves, undermine the development of our unique abilities, undermine our ability to be happy. These are some of the things we need to unlearn:

Competitiveness: Instead of seeing others as fellow beings, we learn suspicion and deception. Competing for grades is our main goal, and in our race for grades there is more and more cheating — destroying the trust that is so necessary for a culture.

Consumerism: Our style of learning is basically one of consuming — we devour the experts' ideas without even digesting them.

We go to school so we can get high-paying jobs in order to have enough money to consume without limits. And we become the world's ultimate consumers, destroying the planet. Education has become a form of consuming where you get what you pay for — students have come to see themselves as paying customers, demanding good grades for their money.

Commercialization: When everything is for sale, nothing is sacred. We have sold our souls. Education has become a commodity and the "quality" of the service you get depends on how much you can pay, just as in medicine or legal representation.

Careerism without conscience: All of these are expressed in the goals of our educational system — choosing a career because of the amount of money and power you'll acquire. Underneath, almost all education focuses on helping people in their race to get the most prestigious, best-paid jobs.

Caste system: Our education system reflects the main society and has produced a caste system. People learn to know their place, and those on the top learn to scorn those beneath them. This produces bitterness and hatred between the levels of society. The people at bottom resent the people at the top, and the people at the top fear those at the bottom. The people at the top are taught that they're special, and they learn to disdain people in the slower reading groups. People who are disdained feel it, and they resent it. This is reflected by Rick Santorum, one of the 2012 Republican presidential candidates, calling President Obama a "snob" for wanting everyone to go to college.

Cynicism: Education should enliven and enlighten, but it makes people cynical because they have no ideals to work for other than the diminished goals of fame and money.

Closemindedness: My experience with the highly educated is that they often do not want to consider any ideas not stamped as worthy by the academy. (Think of the earlier story of historian David Tyack.) Think of how most medical students learn to view alternative health strategies.

Corporatization of life: Philosopher Ivan Illich talks about the institutionalization of our lives — everything is taken away from the individual or the family or the community and given to the experts or authorities. Thus, people no longer educate their children, have family prayers, handle health issues, fix their appliances, grow their own food, make their own music, or entertain themselves. There is an "industry" for each of those: the entertainment industry, the agricultural industry, etc.

Community Education as Living Room Learning

So, in community education we are rebelling against an educational experience that has been corporatized. Based on my experience in getting my doctorate in education at Stanford, it's not too strong to call higher education an experience of anonymity, coldness, regulations, sterility, hypocrisy, boredom, conformity, and dehumanization — which is how I would also describe the corporation.

People want to liberate themselves from overt and covert oppression that keeps them from living fully. Much of people's education deals with freeing people from oppression. The poor Black people in the citizenship schools learned that they had a right to be free and equal. They knew they were oppressed. But how many of us in the educated classes understand that we are also oppressed in many ways? Are we really free and equal? There are many ways that we are kept from living with joy and happiness, so many that we don't even realize. We settle for less, because all we've ever known is less.

My vision is of people gathered together all over the country in our living rooms — all addressing the big questions: How do we live fully? What is our country doing to help us live fully? How is it hindering us? How can we create a supportive culture? We need soul searching.

We need to recreate citizenship schools in our living rooms. We ourselves need to learn how to become citizens. What can we do today that can come anywhere near what those citizenship schools did? How can we help build a movement that will defeat the forces of our corporate, consumer society that are killing the planet and destroying everything that is decent and honorable?

Chapter 9

Study Circles — The People's Think Tanks

*A nation can be maintained only if, between the state
and the individual, there is interposed a whole series of
secondary groups near enough to the individuals to attract
them strongly in their sphere of action and drag them,
in this way, into the general torrent of civil life.*

— Emile Durkheim

Imagine this: Sitting around a dining room table littered with cups and the remains of banana bread are seven or eight people. A burst of laughter dies down as a woman continues her story about trying to persuade her 16-year-old son to wear a helmet when he rides his bike. A man wipes tears of laughter from his eyes and nods vigorously. "Yes, I know just what you mean. My son did that, too. But I read an article the other day that said...."

These people are engaged in one of the most fulfilling human pastimes — conversation. But they're not at a dinner party. They're part of a study circle. In our thrill-seeking, high-tech, hectic times, people are turning to a relaxed, simple, low-tech form of fulfillment and are educating themselves in an informal, egalitarian setting. In our angry and spiteful times, people are turning to a collaborative, caring activity. In our crazy time of hostility to reason and civil discourse, people are turning to a cooperative form of reflection that helps them learn from their own experience, make conscious choices for a happier life, and work for change.

What could better embody our vision of informed citizens coming to together to ponder life's questions than the study circle?

Study circles come to us from Sweden, where they were used in the 19th century to create a democracy that is today admired around the world (and ranked as one of the happiest in the world). In fact, Sweden has been called a "study circle democracy" because study circles are still popular, with one third of adults having participated in one. In effect, research has found that people who participate in a study circle are more likely to get civically involved. Sweden has institutional-ized a system of "thinking, talking, and taking action." (Study circles are subsidized by the government.)

I was thrilled to discover, though, that study circles first came from the United States, where they were used in the early days of the Chautauqua movement, a system of self-edu-cation that was started by churches to educate Sunday school teachers. The movement was expanded by women in the 19th century who were not allowed to go to college but who wanted to educate themselves. (I love to think of those early women coming together for discussions and self education.)

Now, to a lot of people, a study circle doesn't sound very exciting. Over the years people have said, don't call it a *study* circle (a comment on our schooling). But this is what it's been called in Sweden, where it brought about tremendous changes in, it should be noted, a non-violent manner.

I also have reservations about the word circle, because it sounds a little new agey. But when you think about it, the *circle* is a wonderful symbol of the way we should live life — it's a nonhierarchical, congenial way of gathering. When we sit in rows facing forward, as we do in most public gatherings, it's much less of a participatory experience. The circle calls to mind the old idea of the campfire, with people gathered together to keep warm and to comfort each other in a dark, cold night.

We may not be sitting around the campfire much these days, but life can still feel cold and dark. And so we need to come together in our living rooms and gather in a circle to talk, bringing warmth and comfort to each other. (Earlier I referred to E.O. Wilson's book *The Social Conquest of Earth*, in which he talks about the evolutionary path that favored people who could cooperate in groups. He says this began when they first came together in a campsite.)

All that said, you'll have to decide whether to use the word "study circle." I think it should depend on the group. In a school setting maybe it's good, but maybe not in a neighborhood setting. I've also called them conversation circles, community conversation circles, community circles, or community conversations. You need to decide what feels comfortable and appropriate.

In any case, gathering together in small groups for conversation is one of the most transformative experiences you can have. We've been talking about creating a new collaborative culture in which people care about the common good. We've seen that as human beings we're capable of being caring and cooperative if we create institutions and systems that encourage this behavior.

Study circles fit the bill. They are collaborative and cooperative experiences in which we learn to care about others as well as ourselves. To learn to be collaborative and cooperative we need to participate in collaborative and cooperative experiences. You can't learn cooperation and collaboration from a book or a lecture or in a top-down, highly controlled, punitive environment. Most things we do at school and work are pretty much top down. So we learn by doing.

Further, Rebecca Costa, in her book *The Watchman's Rattle: Thinking Our Way Out of Extinction* (2010), cites research showing that the best solutions to problems come from relaxed, congenial small groups. The small-group approach is more effective than either solitary thinking or competitive, judgmental small groups.

Finally, lately I've begun to think of study circles as "the people's think tanks." I've read that our authoritarian right-wing resurgence in the past several years can — in part — be attributed to the conservative think tanks funded by the right-wing billionaires. Obviously they were successful. We'll never have the same amount of money, and we want our efforts to be "of the people, by the people, and for the people." So let's think of them as "the people's think tanks."

Organization of the Material

This material was difficult to organize. There are so many important things about the study circle on so many levels. But I didn't want to heap all the information on you at once. I wanted to present it bit by bit, tantalizing you, arousing your appetite for more. As I wrote, I saw myself moving in ever-widening circles to try to make the case for the study circle.

The material is divided into two chapters: first an explanation of the philosophy of the study circle, second an example of a specific circle — a happiness study circle.

Study Circle Philosophy

First, let me give you a bare sketch of how it works. Six to eight people gather in a living room, tea cups or wine glasses in hand. Three questions guide the evening. The first question asks people to describe their own experience — tell their story. The second question asks them to think critically about their culture. The third involves brainstorming actions, making plans for personal as well as public actions. People talk by going around the circle, taking turns answering the questions, using a congenial and convivial style of conversation. It's conversation, not discussion. There are no contests to win; you're weaving ideas together. In fact, in the first session, participants review the characteristics of good conversation — being interested, supportive, non-argumentative, and non-competitive.

Study circles can be used for any subject because the structure is simple. Because everyone is equal, both teacher and learner, you don't need any special training. There's usually a person who is excited about this idea and wants to start one and sets things up. But that person needs no training, only enthusiasm.

Let's remind ourselves again of our purpose and direction: creating the collaborative society. So how does a study circle help us do that?

Let me start with a work I referred to in the first chapter, Yochai Benkler's *The Penguin and the Leviathan*. I think his ideas help show the significance of the study circle. He argues that if we want the best of people — the most creativity and collaboration — we need certain things. We have to move away from hierarchy and control. People must feel valued and trusted. They must be given a chance to participate and feel a part of something larger than themselves — ideas parallel to our ideas on connection, calling, celebration, and control.

Benkler says that too many of our institutions assume that everyone is selfish and that the only way to motivate people is through rewards or punishments. When we build systems like that, they become self-fulfilling and so people behave in a selfish way. On the other hand, when people are a part of systems that bring out their better nature, they begin to see themselves as cooperative people and they cooperate even more. It sets up a different kind of self-fulfilling prophecy.

Benkler argues that to build a collaborative culture we need to create systems that have these qualities: informality, autonomy, social engagement, inclusion, empathy, solidarity, common purpose, collaboration, moral standards, communication, fairness, intrinsic interest, and trust.

Benkler's list of collaborative qualities is practically a definition of study circles.

Informality — people gathering in living rooms with coffee and tea, seated in a circle, starting the evening with casual, convivial conversation. No lectures, grades, tests, or teachers. There's just a coordinator who gets things started. Why is informality important? Because when things are formal it means there are rules, and usually only a few people know what they are. Formality supports a sort of class structure.

For years the formal structure of Roberts Rules of Order kept me quiet. I always figured I'd say something wrong and people would jump on me. A formal structure like this means that people can't really relax and express themselves freely — they're worried they'll do something to make fools of themselves by breaking one of the invisible rules. Formality makes most people nervous and on their guard — not something that builds trust and solidarity.

Autonomy — the people being in charge. There are study circle guidelines, but essentially this is a participatory experience with people making the decisions about what they want to talk about. There is a general philosophy about study circles, but you can do what you want.

Social engagement — the result of talking in a collaborative manner. This is the lure for people — really getting to talk to real people about real things. It's rare we get to have this quality of a conversation, and it gets people excited about further engagement in the wider society.

Inclusion — feeling you belong. Because the group is small, no one is left out. You begin by taking turns going around the circle to comment, so everyone gets to talk. I've found that the best size is six to eight people. It's like a comfortable dinner party.

Empathy — identifying with the other. This is at the heart of a study circle. People talk about their experiences, not just abstract ideas. It's not a therapy group, but when people get to talk honestly, not worried about what people will think, you begin to have a sense of something in common with them. You come to care about them. You identify with them.

Solidarity — experiencing collective action. I find this is an interesting word for Benkler to use. But yes, people like to feel they belong and that they share values and goals with others. Somehow you feel more protected and safe. Study circle members share a sense that "they're all in this together."

Common purpose — having a shared sense of meaning. Study circles ultimately exist to create a more collaborative and caring culture. There's usually a group goal that people share as well — things like learning to live more simply, learning to be happier. They're not in competition for these things — they're helping each other work toward their individual goals. At the same time, they learn that to change society they must all work together.

Collaboration — working together in a congenial manner. Conversation is the most collaborative activity there is. By sharing our stories, we reduce the competitiveness of people needing to prove how smart they are. No tests or grades. Just a group of people talking together and brainstorming together for new ideas.

Moral standards — understanding the importance of caring for others. Again, this seems a strange factor to bring up. But maybe it's at the heart of things: these study circles exist to create a more caring culture concerned about the common good. That's their purpose in Sweden and that's their purpose here. These aren't investment groups or bridge groups — there is a moral purpose behind them.

Communication — the underlying factor in all of human life. Obviously, you're learning to communicate in a collaborative fashion — you take turns going around the circle. And you're learning how to be a good communicator so you can carry your skills out into the rest of your life. The point is, in a circle everyone gets a chance to talk, and that's not what usually happens these days. And you can't become a better communicator unless you practice.

Fairness — one of the central factors of *caring*. At the heart of the circle is fairness. People are equal. There's no rank; everyone is a teacher as well as a learner; everyone gets equal time to talk; everyone gets respect. Everyone feels heard. Participants don't go away thinking, "It's not fair, Bob got to do all the talking."

Intrinsic interest — everyone wants to be there. No one gets paid to come; no one gets a certificate. Participants are there only because they want to be. The research shows that happiness is directly linked to intrinsic interest, and when you think about it, it's not often we get to act on our intrinsic interests. We're always doing something for some other reason — for money, to be healthy, to get ahead. We need to do more things just because we enjoy them.

In particular, if we compare the idea of learning in the study circle to learning in schools, there's often very little intrinsic interest in learning in schools. You're there for a grade or to qualify yourself for a job.

Trust — the feeling that you can count on others. Apparently this is one of the key ingredients that we need for a caring society. We need to trust our institutions, our politicians, and each other. Societies ultimately won't work if there's no trust. And certainly, this kind of trust has been on the decline.

You have to begin by learning to trust others. As people tell their stories and people accept them, they learn to *trust each other* and feel *connected* and *cared for*. Whenever we say something personal, we're taking a risk. But when you take that risk and you receive support, as you do in a study circle, you learn to trust and care for the other person. In a study circle you treat people with respect; you listen; you don't lie; you don't run down people behind their backs. This is how trust grows.

Study circles, then, are a *methodology*, based on conversation, that will help us build a new culture of caring and collaboration because it is a methodology that *evokes* caring and collaboration. As linguist George Lakoff says, filling people with facts will not bring about progressive ideals. To bring about progressive ideals we need to evoke empathy. You do that by bringing people together to think together, talk together, and take action.

You do this with *congenial* conversation. We're not trying to come up with any decisions or plan any actions together. We're just exploring our lives. No need for arguments or attacks. It's a pleasant evening of good talk and lots of laughter.

Study Circle Methodology

Now you have the basic philosophy. Let's see what actually happens in a study circle. Let's say the topic for the evening is *community*. Remember, the evening's conversation revolves around three questions.

First question: *When in your life have you experienced community? And what does community mean to you?* People tell their stories — about student housing in grad school, being in a babysitting co-op, working for a political cause, or even taking the same bus to work every day. As they tell their stories, a definition of community emerges, and people begin to understand its importance. As people talk about these life experiences, you can feel the energy rise. They're talking about real things. Real emotions emerge. This is how people connect.

Second question: *What are the forces in our culture that make community difficult?* People talk about not having enough time, about competitiveness at work, about the focus on appearance and status, about the pressure to succeed. As they tell their stories and realize how much they have in common, they begin to see the forces in our culture that make community difficult. Themes emerge, and participants realize that this is bigger than their own lives.

Third question: *What actions can you take to increase community in your life?* People brainstorm personal actions such as joining a neighborhood group, working for a political cause, or just having a neighborhood potluck. After brainstorming, each person commits to taking an action, and in the next session, they report to the group. As they talk about actions, they begin to realize we also need larger institutional changes. At this point they talk about the need for policies on things like guaranteed vacations, sick leave, and parental leave. They see the need for community centers and libraries and parks. They begin to talk about ways to bring about long-term change for policies on matters such as wealth equality.

So the study circle has three basic focuses: understanding our own experience, learning from each other about cultural forces, and taking action for personal and public change. Let's explore the importance of these

Understanding Our Own Experience

Many years ago I heard a Native American tell about his education growing up. He said his grandfather would take him into the woods and leave him there to watch — maybe beavers building a dam, birds flitting through the trees, whatever was there. At the end of the day his grandfather would return and ask him three questions: What did you observe? What did you feel? What did you learn? When I heard his story I knew that this should be the basis of all of our learning — learning from our own experiences. We're bombarded by so many ideas; how else would we choose which one to follow than by looking at what we have learned from life?

If we are going to make good decisions, we must learn to reflect on our experience. Much of what we do is *what we're expected to do*. We're following someone else's ideas. We behave the way others want out of fear of negative consequences or to get positive reinforcement. At some level, we all want to fit in. We absorb the cultural rules without even knowing it. We take actions that are not necessarily in our own best interests (or in the interests of people and the planet).

But we can make good decisions only if we reflect on our experience. We have to ask ourselves, What did I observe? What did I feel? What did I learn? As I outlined earlier, we're learning to listen to our still, small, inner voice that is too often buried or ignored. It's about discerning wisdom, one of the most important human abilities, and it's based on reflecting on our own experience — asking ourselves what we've learned and then making conscious choices.

It's the "examined life" that wise people have always advocated. In her book *Twelve Steps to a Compassionate Life*, Karen Armstrong explores the beliefs of Socrates, Buddha, and Confucius. They believed that knowledge is a process of self-discovery, that people find the truth within themselves, that if people looked into their own minds, they would find they have the answers they are searching for. (We can see that this is what we mean by *soul searching*.) Further, that this happens best when you have someone listening to you closely and in an accepting way. Armstrong says that Confucius always developed his insights in conversation with other people; Socrates explored ideas by asking others questions; Buddha taught his monks to converse in a kindly fashion with each other. All wise people have advocated looking within.

Learning from Each Other about Cultural Forces

Early in the women's movement I gathered weekly with other women in small groups and we told each other our stories about having boyfriends, getting married, worrying about our appearance, feeling like we were dumb, getting divorced, and on and on. And always the same themes emerged — we all doubted ourselves; we all thought we weren't good enough, that we needed to be married to be complete. But in talking with each other, we realized that it wasn't something wrong with us. It was the invisible cultural forces controlling us which we learned to identify as sexism. We had all unconsciously learned what it meant to be female, how to act and feel as a woman, and finally the rules were becoming conscious. We felt liberated, and we changed.

Part of learning about our own experiences is understanding the forces in our society that affect us. There are not only unspoken rules about how to act as a woman or a man, there are rules about how to act as an American or a young person or a white person. Without understanding these rules, it's like having an inaccurate map to find a destination. It's hard to see these cultural forces because they look *so normal*. We unconsciously absorbed them as we grew up. It seemed normal to women to not have a career. It seemed normal to quit work when you had a baby. It seemed normal to do all the cooking and the child care. Then we starting asking, Who says? In the early days of the women's movement it was called *consciousness raising*. It took someone like Betty Friedan to call it "the problem that has no name." Then women started talking to each other and comparing notes, beginning to understand the cultural forces of gender expectations.

In study circles, we can discover the unconscious rules that are influencing us today.

Taking Action for Personal and Public Change

For years I led simplicity circles, small groups that helped people live more simply. Everyone wanted to break out of the cultural trance of consumerism, but as research shows, we become like the people we're around. Earlier I referred to the authors Christakis and Fowler and their book *Connected: The Surprising Power of Our Social Networks and How They Shape Our Lives.* These authors show how much influence our social networks have on us in our health and happiness and even our weight. In essence, we need to pick the people we want to be like and spend time with them.

Study circles help us make conscious changes by discussing them with the group. Actions are always more successful when we receive support and encouragement from others. Being with others who share our values helps us advance in the directions we choose.

We really learn something only by testing it out, so after *reflecting*, we must *act*, and then reflect some more. Action is part of learning. Too often in our schools what we "learn" is not applied to our lives. We're not encouraged to act on it. In fact, we're supposed to be "objective" and *not* apply things to our own lives. I remember how the professors would discourage anything personal in my college classes — even in my classes on *women's* literature. For me, reading novels was all about learning how to live. Certainly, we need to try out our ideas by taking action on them.

So we take action and then we come back to report to others and talk things over with them, gaining new insights.

The study circle embodies the goals of community education because it helps us talk, think, and take action.

Significance of the Study Circle Structure

Now let's take a look at the significance of the way the questions are structured.

First Question: When in Your Life Have You Experienced Community?

The question is structured to undermine the competitiveness that we learned in our classrooms: our education has trained us to compete and engage in conflict with each other. It becomes automatic to try to poke holes in others' arguments, to point out weaknesses and flaws in others' reasoning. But attacks just close minds, making people resistant to new ideas. How do we get people to converse differently?

Well, maybe we can *tell* people to behave differently and give them discussion *guidelines* to follow. But that's not enough. We automatically revert to our competitive ways. We automatically start debating when an idea comes up. We have to structure things differently.

The study circle doesn't rely just on *telling* people to avoid debate and attack; no, it is *structured in a manner that undermines competitiveness because it asks people to take turns telling their own stories.* Instead of debating ideas, study circle members share their own experiences. There's nothing to debate. It's a personal story. The circle helps people explore and take control of their own lives by the way it is structured — focusing on personal stories, not just ideas.

One of the most valuable things about telling personal stories is that people connect with each other. In most settings, we debate ideas and rarely reveal anything personal, so we don't really get to know each other. In fact, because we're encouraged to try to attack and win, we become wary of each other, failing to build trust.

SELF-KNOWLEDGE

When we tell our own stories, we say things that surprise ourselves, things we didn't even know we were thinking.

Self-knowledge seems to require talking with others. What the other person says sparks something new within us and we build on that, and we respond in like manner. Just thinking by ourselves doesn't seem to be enough. So, as we tell our stories, we gain in self-knowledge and self-acceptance. We realize that we have never really liked cooking, and that's OK. We realize that we never really liked to shop for clothes, and that's OK (in fact, more than OK). We realize that we're messy and disorganized, and that's OK! Self-acceptance, a building block of collegiality, only comes from self-knowledge.

If we're going to make good decisions in our lives, we need to know ourselves, and self-knowledge seems to require self-revelation. Because the circle is safe, people get a chance to say things they've never said before, and it's exhilarating to drop the social mask and be yourself.

SELF-TRUST

It's hard to reveal ourselves because, at some level, we're all worried that people will laugh at us or reject us. But when we tell people our embarrassing stories — like dressing wrong for a fancy wedding or tripping as we walked on stage — we lose our worry. It's only when we're hiding ourselves that we worry about what others think. When we take the risk to be honest, we begin to trust ourselves.

When we tell our own stories, we move beyond the second-hand ideas that we get from experts. We develop our own values and learn to trust our own judgment. Until we really pay attention to our experiences and how we feel about them, we are trapped by conventional thinking.

As we begin to think our own thoughts, we begin to trust our own judgment. We don't have to go along with the crowd. We don't have to take a job in a bank. We don't have to buy a new car. We can live in a tiny house or join Zipcar or plant a garden in our front yard. We're free!

We *can* challenge the experts. Too often we think that other people know what they're talking about, that other people are

confident in their ideas; so we let ourselves be influenced —
on everything from evaluating movies to evaluating political
candidates. One study showed a group of people a picture of
a number of lines of different length. The "plant" in the group
claimed the middle line was the longest, even though it wasn't.
Everyone went along with it.

But once we have the experience of discerning and expressing our true feelings, we trust them more. We develop a *clarity*
about what we want out of life and go our own way.

INCREASED CONFIDENCE

Study circle participants learn confidence in expressing themselves — something few of us feel confident in doing these
days in our competitive culture. Not only are they learning that
they can think for themselves, but they're also learning to speak
up and express themselves. This is because they're in a safe setting. The rules of a circle are the rules of good conversation: no
attacking, no trying to win an argument. They're there to tell
their own stories and listen to others. They're there to support
each person in finding their way. This is how people learn confidence — by being listened to in a supportive manner.

EQUALITY

Maybe the best lesson we get is that we understand that we're
equals. Benkler focuses on fairness as being an essential trait
of collaboration, and equality is an essential part of fairness.
Whenever there's inequality, there is some resentment, a sense
of being "on guard." There's the feeling we had when we were
little: It's not fair. He got more.

Equality is the basis of self-respect and respect of others. As
I've said before (and obviously will keep on saying), in unequal
societies everything suffers; there is lower life expectancy, more
depression, drug addiction, crime, etc. It's because inequality
destroys social cohesion. The struggle for status hurts us because
we're always playing a game, a game to protect ourselves and
take down the other. If we've never experienced equality, how

will we know how it feels? Will we even recognize it when we see it? Will we even value it?

When people tell their own stories, they relate as *equals* because the more highly educated are unable to dominate by quoting facts and figures and current ideas. In fact, the highly educated often are not as effective in telling their own stories because they've never done it — self-revelation is frowned upon in the academic life. They've masked themselves behind abstract ideas and studies. They've learned to act important.

Once you've experienced equality and understand its importance, you'll always expect it.

Second Question: What Forces in Our Culture Affect Community?

The first question encourages us to look at our own lives. The second question encourages us to think critically about our society. We have to remember that at one time people accepted ideas we now find abhorrent: they accepted slavery, indentured servants, inequality for women, and on and on. Most people accepted them as normal, and it took people questioning things to bring about change. In fact, I often wonder if people in the future will think about inequality in wealth as being as barbaric as other forms of inequality.

As people talk about their difficulties in creating community, they observe that they are coming up with many of the same reasons. They begin to understand that there are powerful cultural forces affecting them (for instance, competition, no time, no public spaces). It's not just an individual problem. Their difficulties aren't their fault.

When we see life only in individualistic terms, we miss half the picture. We're operating from a faulty map of reality until we understand the cultural forces acting on us.

Further, a personal view of change is very limiting. Americans tend to see life in terms of the individual, so when things go wrong, we blame ourselves and feel powerless. When we realize *it's not our fault* — that there are strong cultural forces out there — we feel liberated and galvanized for action. This "consciousness raising" has always played a role in movements for social change. As Myles Horton, founder of Highlander said, when people begin to see reality, they can develop truly effective methods for change.

Third Question: What Actions Can You Take to Build Community?

There are two aspects to consider: personal actions and public change.

PERSONAL ACTIONS

Too often we read about problems but we're not given any ideas about taking action, leaving us feeling powerless. So we need suggestions. However, people often argue over whether we should focus on personal change or public change. We need both. We probably need to start with the personal because, even though we ultimately want broad cultural change, starting with personal actions motivates us to take larger actions. Taking personal action provides information about how ideas will work. Things often work differently in real life than in theory.

Study circles are very helpful for personal change: You are more likely to make changes when you tell others about your plans. You're more likely to act when you have the support of others. You're more likely to act when you know your friends are waiting to hear how it went. In the study circle you learn that small actions are more likely to succeed, that doing things you enjoy is more effective, that taking action gives you feelings of control in your life.

PUBLIC CHANGE

This is where we begin to solve the underlying problems of our culture. For instance, when we talk about community we might talk about how to change wealth inequality because it affects social cohesion. We realize that we need to take the money out of election campaigns. We realize that we need policies that make it easier for people to vote. As we explore public change, we begin to discover our calling, and we incorporate both personal and public change.

When we generate ideas about social change, we begin to feel a part of something larger than ourselves — perhaps the most gratifying feeling of all. As Benkler said, we need systems that give us solidarity and a sense of purpose. This a study circle does.

Now let me show you exactly how one works with a description of a community happiness circle.

Chapter 10

The Happiness Circle: From the Pursuit of Happiness to Gross Domestic Happiness

It is through solving problems in accordance with the highest light that we have that inner growth is attained. Now, collective problems must be solved by us collectively, and no one finds inner peace who avoids doing his or her share in the solving of collective problems.

— Peace Pilgrim

A Focus on Happiness

Whenever I tell people I'm leading a "happiness circle," I feel a little embarrassed. That's strange, really, because happiness is our basic goal in life. It's probably because the idea of happiness has been diminished — we associate it with phony inspirational speakers telling us to look on the bright side of life, to keep a smile on our faces. They don't talk about the sources of our anxieties and despair — the destruction of the planet, the people who are hungry around the world, the people in prison who don't deserve to be there. Real reasons to be worried.

So talking about happiness is difficult because it's been approached in a shallow, superficial way. So why talk about it then? Because maybe it's the only way to get people to talk about values and ideals. We're not likely to get a lot of people to a study circle on world poverty. There are a few of us who might be excited about that, but we need to find a way to engage the "average" person, the everyday citizen.

Essentially it's important to talk about happiness *because our misunderstanding of happiness is responsible for many of our problems.* In particular, the belief that being rich will make you happy means that *anything goes* in the pursuit of profit, even if it undermines the well-being of people or the planet. In the circle we explore the new research about happiness, helping people understand the cultural misconceptions about happiness. As we've grown up, we have learned the wrong ideas about happiness, and there's little hope until we truly understand it.

There are two segments to happiness circles. The first segment focuses on *personal* happiness. It's important to engage people by starting where they are — helping them change their personal lives. The idea that they can be happier is what draws people in.

But as they talk together we need to help people realize that personal change is not enough, and that we need *public* policies. Thus, for the second segment we explore the ideas embodied in the Gross National Happiness movement.

Personal Happiness

In this first segment of the happiness circle, we talk about the basic elements of personal happiness — *community, calling, celebration,* and *control.*

Session One: Community and Conversation

At the beginning of the first meeting, introduce the idea of congenial conversation. People need to be reminded that they are having a convivial conversation and not a competitive discussion. Ask people to gather in small groups and list the attributes of a good conversation and a bad conversation. Encourage people to see that the conversation circle will use good conversation techniques of listening, taking turns, and affirming each other while avoiding anger, attack, ranting and raving. Further, avoid being negative about everything. People will just get sick of you. Yes, there's lots that's wrong, but remember that, as a group, you're searching for positive actions to take.

Periodically during the eight weeks, stop and review the techniques of good conversation.

After exploring conversation, begin to discuss the three questions related to that week's factor of happiness.

1. Research finds that social ties are the most important factor in happiness, so the first question explores experience with relationships: *When in your life have you experienced support-ive community and a sense of belonging?*

    Go around the circle and tell your stories. Limit each person to three minutes. One person can be a time keeper or you can use an old fashioned egg timer where the sand takes three minutes to run through. (You need two of them — if someone doesn't take the full three minutes, you don't want to have to wait for the sand to run through before the next person starts.) Try to discern what the common factors of community are. Consider college dorms, sports, commutes on buses, political actions and then think about shared values, acceptance, support, availability, caring, etc.

2. Further, research finds that social ties are on the decline, so the next question asks you to explore the larger cultural factors affecting you: *What forces in society make it difficult for you to have community?*

    Consider working hours, television, the Internet, long commutes, the media, social media, fast-paced lives, large houses, lack of gathering places, the wealth gap.

3. Finally, there are lots of things we can do to begin to con-nect with others, so the third question helps people commit to an action: *What short-term and long-term actions can you take to introduce more community into your life?*

    Participants should announce what they will do that week and be prepared to give a report the next meeting. Consider getting to know neighbors, taking up a hobby, joining a club, getting involved with politics, joining a church, having friends over for dinner. At the beginning of the next session, have a "check in" to report on the actions taken.

Session Two: Calling

Remember to begin with a "check in," reporting on the actions taken to build community. Then proceed to address the questions in the same manner as last time.

1. An important factor in happiness is having something that gives you a sense of direction and meaning, something that absorbs you and engages you. So the first question asks you to look at your experience to see what brings a sense of excitement, something that "calls out" to you: *Is there a time in your life when you were (or are) really excited about something — something that seemed to call out to you and call on your abilities, something that gave you a sense of purpose and meaning?*

   Consider experiences of volunteering, being active in politics, becoming involved in the arts, being totally absorbed in something.

2. We've come to believe that wealth and status are more important than meaning. Many factors in our culture have led us to focus on getting ahead and impressing people: *What forces in society have made it difficult to pursue a calling?*

   Consider the focus in schools to pass tests, the pressure to keep up with the Joneses, the expectation to earn lots of money and consume, the lack of unscheduled time as kids grow up, the shortage of leisure time because of long working hours.

3. Having begun the meeting by having a "check in" and reporting on actions taken, now focus on action that can be taken to identify calling: *What short- and long-term actions could you take to explore your calling?*

   Consider taking a class, going to lectures, reading newspapers, joining a club, talking to new people, reading widely, getting involved in politics, volunteering, taking up old hobbies.

Session Three: Celebration

1. Even with friends and a sense of meaning, it's easy to feel overwhelmed and anxious and to seek distraction from boredom by watching television or working long hours. We need to learn to live with a sense of celebration, to enjoy even the little things in our lives: *In what ways do you enjoy your day-to-day life?*

   Consider sports, the arts, singing, dancing, getting together with friends, living in a leisurely fashion, taking reflective time to appreciate good things. Consider rituals and habits that build *joie de vivre.*

2. We live in a culture that is concerned about wealth, not people. We don't always feel supported and valued. We're worried about financial and physical health. It's easy to blame ourselves, but when we do, we're less likely to take action for change. Sometimes we just feel guilty because we have more than others. All these factors undermine our ability to enjoy life, so we need to consider the outside forces: *What forces in society have made it difficult to enjoy life?*

   Consider money worries, stress about unemployment, long working hours, amount of time spent on the Internet or watching television, violence, guns, lack of public health care, worry about the environment, few public places to gather, our extreme individualism.

3. To bring about real change, we need to take specific action: *What short- or long-term actions could you take to enjoy your life more?*

   Consider activities people might get involved in that bring joy: taking time over meals, taking daily walks and stopping to chat with neighbors, taking naps, going to plays and movies, slowing down and learning to appreciate life, going to flash mobs or demonstrations, joining a group to save the environment.

Session Four: Control

1. Happiness research finds that when we feel out of control of our lives, we feel less happy. A feeling of control involves many different aspects in terms of living in ways that we choose — from financial health to physical and emotional health: *In what ways do you feel that your life is out of your control?*

   Consider lack of savings, credit card debt, clutter, feeling rushed, feeling it's difficult to influence the government, having a dictatorial boss.

2. Again, we berate ourselves for failing to carry through on our resolutions for change. We need to understand the forces against us so that we can mobilize for real change: *What cultural forces make it difficult to feel in control?*

   Consider long work hours, cultural pressure to consume (e.g., commercials on television), Protestant work ethic, individualism (which discourages turning to others for help), a cruel economy, pressure to eat junk foods.

3. Finally, there are individual things we can do, but the real answer often involves coming together in solidarity to work together for change. The experience in the circle allows us to learn how to collaborate and work with others. It's important to start first with personal change, but be sure to consider collective action as well: *What actions could you take to gain more control over your life?*

   Consider reducing consumerism, joining a local political party precinct, joining a union, getting more sleep, eating in a healthier fashion, walking more, watching less television, taking a class.

Public Policies/Gross National Happiness

In the second segment of happiness circles, discuss ideas from the Gross National Happiness (GNH) movement — the idea of going beyond measuring progress by the Gross National Product, which measures only money. It's a commitment to measuring quality of life as well. (Read more about this and take the GNH survey at http://happycounts.org/survey/GNH.)

Although there are several factors in the GNH, at this point we consider only three, summing things up with a conversation on democracy.

In earlier sessions you have talked about long-term solutions; in these sessions you can begin to bring together a lot of your ideas from talking, thinking, and taking action.

Session Five: Community Vitality and Social Connection Policies

1. Review your earlier conversation on community. In your experience, what were the most significant forces undermining community?
2. What public policies would bring long-term change? Consider transportation policies (we spend too much time in cars), working hours (we have no time to gather), the architecture of neighborhoods (we have no places to gather), the pressure on children (they have too many commitments), the role of technology (too much screen time).
3. In what ways could you work to support policy changes? Consider joining a local precinct, joining a group like the Sierra Club, writing letters to the newspapers, voting.

Session Six: Work/Time Balance Policies

1. Consider the answers when you talked about control in your life. What are the cultural forces that make you feel harried and hurried? Consider long work hours, commutes, screen time.
2. What public policies could bring long-term changes? Consider regulations on the banks and corporations, policies that reduce the wealth gap, shorter work hours and longer vacations, a safety net of features such as unemployment insurance, health care, mass transit.
3. What strategies could you work on to bring these about? Conversations with friends, writing to newspapers/online groups, joining a political organization, volunteering with a nonprofit organization.

Session Seven: Environmental Quality and Access to Nature Policies

1. What areas of the environment are you particularly concerned about? Consider climate change, air pollution, destruction of the soil, etc.
2. What public policies could bring long-term changes? Consider mass transit, living local, the bicycle culture, solar energy.
3. What strategies could you work on to bring these about? Consider being active in politics, working with 350.org (Bill McKibben's organization working on climate change), becoming involved in the Transition movement.

Session Eight: Democracy

In the final session, wrap things up by connecting all you have talked about to the idea of democracy. Consider Lakoff's words on democracy:

> Democracy, in the American tradition, has been defined by a simple morality: We Americans care about our fellow citizens, we act on that care and build trust, and we do our best not just for ourselves, our families, and our friends and neighbors, but for our country, for each other, for people we have never seen and never will see.
>
> American Democracy has, over our history, called upon citizens to share an equal responsibility to work together to secure a safe and prosperous future for their families and nation. This is the central work of our democracy and it is a public enterprise. This, the American Dream, is the dream of a functioning democracy.

People need to realize the importance of coming together to talk. The American philosopher John Dewey said, "Democracy begins in conversation." Harvard sociologist Robert

Putnam found that when the number of clubs and organizations rose, government was more responsive. Finally, Denmark, a highly democratic country, has been rated the number one happiest country, and 95 percent of its people belong to some form of club or organization. Some are calling this the *social cure!*

Explore this question: *How is democracy strengthened by your participation in this circle?* Consider the following:

- Democracy is strengthened as people gain clarity and confidence about expressing their own opinions. They learn to trust their own judgment rather than rely on conventional sources for ideas.
- When people talk in a safe, non-judgmental place, they learn to express themselves with more confidence, making it more likely that they'll speak up. When they are supported, they are more likely to take action.
- It is people who build movements. Movements start because people talk to each other. When they tell each other what they have experienced, they invariably discover that others have experienced the same thing. People usually think they are alone in what they feel until they tell someone else and discover their commonality. In our individualistic society, we blame ourselves when something is wrong. When people talk to others they come to understand the cultural forces affecting them all.

End the circle by summarizing the actions you plan on continuing to take: *What have been the most important issues in this circle, and how will you go on working for them and for the strengthening of democracy?*

This is the formal end of the circle, but these questions can be explored over and over again. Some circles have lasted for years.

Essentially, you can use this format for any subject. You begin by telling about your experience with an issue — being a parent, being a worker, being an activist, whatever. You can devise the questions.

Next, you discuss the cultural forces that are undermining your efforts for a positive outcome — What makes it hard to be a good parent? What are the anti-democratic forces in the workplace? Whatever.

Finally, you talk about short- and long-term actions. Between sessions you act and return the next week to talk about it.

You do all of this on any topic of your choosing, using the guidelines of good conversation.

FAQ

How often should you meet?

It's best to meet once a week. Not everyone can be there every time, but meeting less often can lead to feeling disconnected and not coming back.

Do you need a trained leader?

No, the structure of the three questions means the gathering can run itself. It's best to have a coordinator who starts things, arranges for the room, etc.

How do you start a group?

It's probably easiest to start a group within another organization such as a church or an environmental group. That gives you access to a targeted audience and a method of communicating through the group's website or email.

You can also put a notice up in a library or community center. Consider proposing a group to a continuing education program at a community college or university.

Should you charge a fee?

No, this is meant to be free and open to everyone.

Where can you meet?

Try libraries, community centers, or churches. Some meet in homes, and there seems to be no problem. People who get involved are usually very nice people. Consider a coffee shop as well, particularly in the beginning. Some groups continue to meet for years, so people's homes might work well here.

Responses to Happiness Circles

Below is a collection of some responses to a happiness circle (slightly edited to remove things that were too personal).

Hello Happiness & Sharing Friends:
It has been a wonderful experience being part of this circle.

You all have helped me launch my personal mission of building community with my neighbors. Each of you brings unique experiences and your own talents to the group. It was a wonderful experience to be with people who are trying to make a positive change in the world. I've really appreciated the ideas and encouragement you've provided me for my neighborhood events. And most importantly, being part of the circle made me accountable to a group of individuals who started out as strangers and over the months became special friends.

I will continue to focus on my Cs — and hope that we can continue to stay in touch and support each other — whether through email or an online group, or an occasional brown-bag lunch on campus.

Hi Everyone!
This group was important to me and I looked forward to it. I came to this group for connection and I liked the topic. I found the group to be very enlightening and comfortable and safe. I learned a lot, and confirmed the importance of some things that I knew. There were some things I needed/wanted to do, and being in a group helped to push me forward and I felt some accountability, as I wanted to be able to report progress to the group. I truly enjoyed hearing what the group members had done each week, and I found the sharing time especially useful. The emails from others were also helpful/useful.

I loved the four Cs, though I could not always remember them, and felt that I made some progress in the areas of community and calling.

Hi Everyone!
Here are my thoughts about the sharing group experience.

I look forward to the meetings every week. The one hour that we spend sharing our stories, ideas, and experiences recharges me in a positive way. An atmosphere of inclusiveness is created by the welcoming and pleasant disposition of the members of the group, which also helps to create an open and safe place to share my thoughts. I don't feel pressure, stress or anxiety in our meetings. We all live busy lives, and I feel the group meetings are great because talking about sharing makes me mindful of it. It allows me to bring sharing to the forefront of my mind so that I am conscious of applying it to my everyday interactions. I have noticed this has happened to me many times since I started participating in the group. After our weekly meeting, I find myself sharing more and applying the ideas from the group to improve my interactions with those around me. As a result, I have started feeling more satisfied with my connections with others.

I hope our paths will cross again, and thank you to everyone for making this a very memorable experience.

Good Morning,
The group was important to me because I am so very isolated, working from dark to dark in my office in front of a computer, trying to meet the needs of the multiple personnel in my department in a timely manner. I allowed myself the treat of getting out to attend your group meeting on Fridays (although not every Friday) to get new ideas within my area of interest and to receive support. I met new people and was stimulated and in awe by all they were trying out and accomplishing. It was one place where I was not treated as weird because I no longer shop as a hobby, I recycle and reuse items instead of buying new, and just do with less.

Hi Everyone,
I really enjoyed the camaraderie of this group, something that is not easy to find in this overly wealthy area. As for this particular group, it was great to get to meet others (and talk about interesting things) in the context of knowing that they also

want more connection in their lives. So now I'll have to think how to stay connected in some way.

Study circles give a context for meeting others around mutual interests that, if intentionally utilized, can spawn new friendships, new neighborly relations, and more of a social support network for each person. This social network, of course, is one of the cornerstones of happiness and life success in the most holistic sense of the word.

I hope I see more of you over the next months somehow (maybe in Transition?). I very much enjoyed getting to know you a bit.

Chapter 11

Dancing in the Streets

Surely joy is the condition of life.
— Henry David Thoreau

i thank You God for most this amazing
day: for the leaping greenly spirits of trees
and a blue true dream of sky; and for everything
which is natural which is infinite which is yes

(i who have died am alive again today,
and this is the sun's birthday; this is the birth
day of life and of love and wings: and of the gay
great happening illimitably earth)

how should tasting touching hearing seeing
breathing any — lifted from the no
of all nothing — human merely being
doubt unimaginable You?

(now the ears of my ears awake and
now the eyes of my eyes are opened)
— ee cummings

I am grateful for what I am and have. My thanksgiving
is perpetual....O how I laugh when I think of my vague
indefinite riches. No run on my bank can drain it, for
my wealth is not possession but enjoyment.

— Henry David Thoreau

> *If the day and the night are such that you greet them with*
> *joy, and life emits a fragrance like flowers and sweet-*
> *scented herbs, is more elastic, more starry, more immortal*
> *— that is your success. All nature is your congratulation,*
> *and you have cause momentarily to bless yourself....*
> *The true harvest of my daily life is somewhat as intangible*
> *and indescribable as the tints of morning or evening.*
> *It is a little star-dust caught, a segment of the rainbow*
> *which I have clutched.*
>
> — Henry David Thoreau

Community Celebrations

My impulse is to follow these quotes with just two words: "Enough said."

These are quotes that I have carried around with me through the years — committing some of them to memory and having them periodically emerge in my mind. Particularly now. The core of this book is that if we are to survive, if we are to avoid destroying the planet and its people, we need to learn to care about each other and the common good. We need a new culture that isn't competitive and cutthroat, that isn't every man for himself. We have to realize that we're all in this together. That we need each other.

There are some things we need to do. We need to help people understand the new, more positive, visions of human nature and happiness. We need to support community, the "sharing revolution," and localization. We need to create a new way of learning and education — community education that is by the people, for the people, and of the people, and we can use a very special tool that brings people together in equality and empathy, the study circle. And it's all supported by conversation — caring, lively, egalitarian conversation.

We need to engage people, but we must do everything in a wider context; it's not just *what* we do but the *way* we do it. If we want people to care for the common good, there are certain emotions we must evoke; there are certain experiences people must have. In particular, we've seen that we must evoke empathy — the idea that caring for the common good means caring for people you don't even know. Empathy is an emotion that connects you to others, helps you see life through their eyes. We've seen that empathy comes through all sorts of community activities like "stop and chats," study circles, and sharing your tools.

But all of these things can be done in a half-hearted way. Too many people just go through the motions with no enthusiasm; or they come to gatherings to rant and rave, attacking people who don't agree with them. Even in public gatherings we can give in to doom and gloom.

The necessary emotion is joy. As we learned from the story of the San Francisco earthquake, we need to learn *joy in the other fellow*. We must have more than community. It must be joyful community.

Why is joy so important? Because to inspire people to bring about change — to work to create a culture of caring — we need the strongest, most motivating emotion there is, and joy is the ultimate experience of happiness, the essential desire of our lives. We are a depressed, cynical, lonely people, and only joy will move us. On a personal level we're isolated and unhappy; on a national level we're so divided by hostility that our government is paralyzed. Not only is civic responsibility declining, there's a decline in any kind of group activity. We have no sense of mutual responsibility, no joy of solidarity. And solidarity is all we have to use against the powers that be.

We must inspire people to come together. To paraphrase Antoine de St. Exupery, the author of *The Little Prince*, if you want someone to build you a boat, you don't just give them tools, wood, and plans; no, you teach them to yearn for the vast and endless sea. We can't just shake a finger at people. We have to give people a vision of the joyful life so that they'll throw themselves into its creation.

How do we do this? We need the equivalent of what Barbara Ehrenreich has described as "dancing in the streets."

In her book of that name, she discovers that as civilization has advanced, people quit dancing in the streets. Dancing in the streets is something real that people used to do, but it's also a symbol — a symbol of communal joy. Ehrenreich says that people in power realize that people who dance in the streets are people you can't control — so it's gradually driven out of the culture. Ehrenreich does a fascinating job of tracing the rise of civilization and the demise of the experience of collective joy. As capitalism rose, joyful ecstasy fell. In particular, the people at the top learned to look at the joyful dancing of the "primitive" people as something disgusting. Disgust and disdain are tools the powerful use to control the underlings. Feeling "disrespected" is one of the primary forces behind rage and anger.

Ehrenreich links the decline of ecstatic dancing to the introduction of Calvinism and capitalism. In the 17th century, people were apparently hit with an epidemic of depression — something new to people. Lionel Trilling, a legendary intellectual and literary critic, said that it seemed as though a "mutation of human nature took place." There was a new preoccupation with "the self" — with mirrors, self-portraits, and autobiographies becoming popular. At the same time, people went to events like plays and concerts to be entertained, not to participate as they had done earlier. As the caste system was solidified, people became obsessed with self-presentation and status. And individualism and isolation grew.

Then, in the 19th century there was a rise in suicide. Max Weber, an influential sociologist and political economist, saw this as the rise of Calvinism and capitalism — two ideologies that created an "unprecedented inner loneliness" in a competitive, sink-or-swim economy. You existed to work, not to enjoy yourself with other people. Both Calvinism and capitalism destroyed spontaneous impulsive enjoyment.

This all seemed to occur, argues Ehrenreich, when the class system arose (again wealth inequality). She quotes an anthropologist, Victor Turner, as seeing the dancing of peasants as "an expression of *communitas* — love and solidarity in a community of equals." That is something we no longer have — but it is the vision that we're searching for.

So to create a new culture, we need to create the equivalent of dancing in the streets — people coming together for joyful community, finding joy in the other fellow. This was what we were doing in the '60s. All the movements were centered around music and people dancing and marching to the music. "Dancing in the Streets" was recorded by Martha and the Vandellas in 1964 when the civil rights movement really became visible to the rest of the country. It was in 1964 that northern students went south to work in the movement and everything changed. Lyrics in the song called out, "This is an invitation, across the nation, A chance for folks to meet!" Exactly! Who among us can not feel the lure and excitement of the civil rights movement when we hear the music of the '60s?

We need to reclaim those feelings. It's more than empathy; it's joy in the other fellow. It's what Kay Jamison, in her book *Exuberance: The Passion for Life,* refers to as the "wine of the gods." Exuberance is an ebullient, effervescent emotion that is unrestrained and irrepressible. Pasteur said the Greeks gave us a wonderful word — enthusiasm, "a God within." "Happy is he who bears a God within, and who obeys it," said Pasteur. Jamison asks what happens when the wine runs out. What happens when people no longer care? Depression and loneliness and a loss of connection to others. A decline in happiness.

How can we evoke joy and exuberance?

One thing comes to mind — community celebrations.

Farmers Markets

To me, the closest thing to a community celebration we have is the farmers market. One summer evening my husband and I were in San Luis Obispo, California, heading down to the beach. We discovered that they were having their weekly farmers market, so we stopped in and found a wonderful band playing rock music. There we were, at the beach, with a beautiful evening, the sun sinking in the west, dancing in the streets! It was bliss.

We always discover something like this at a farmers market. There's always live music; there are local farmers whom you get to know; there are crafts, flowers, and people practicing democracy, proffering petitions to be signed. Friends calling out to each other. A perfect place for a stop and chat. In fact, leading environmentalist Bill McKibben claims that we have ten times the number of conversations at a farmers market that we do at regular grocery stores.

Summer Streets

And you can go even further. In Seattle we've started something called Summer Streets. The city closes four or five blocks of the local business district and invites anyone in the community to have an event. Our sustainability group held a "Dancing in the Streets" event in front of our local independent book store. (It wasn't the most successful event, though, because our sound system kept getting stuck and starting over. We listened to Aretha Franklin's "Respect" many, many times.)

The mayor came on his bicycle and helped us sing happy birthday to a friend who had just broken her leg. The "bubble man" was there — a man who blows giant bubbles through hoops made out of recycled goods and talks to kids about the environment. All the shops were open, serving wine and snacks. Bands came. There were booths of crafts. Up and down everyone walked, talking with everyone. Kids played games in the streets, decorated their bicycles, drew colorful chalk pictures, and ate popcorn. People sat at the outdoor café tables, smiling, laughing, and greeting passersby.

Fairs

In Seattle the sustainability movement doesn't have old-fashioned conferences, but rather festivals and fairs held outside with things to look at and people to talk to. In Portland's City Repair project people paint their intersections and populate them with mini libraries, play houses, and benches to sit and chat. Once a year they form a giant circle around the city — a circle of people holding hands.

I could go on, talking about the Green Festivals, Bioneers, and Mother Earth News Fair. Actually, the Mother Earth News Fair is one of my favorites because it's the only time I've given a workshop when the competing workshop was "How to Raise a Healthy Goat." I love looking at the titles of its workshops and exhibits. Besides topics on solar electricity, electric cars, and straw-bale building, there are workshops on tiny homes, chicken whispering, bee keeping, and bow and arrow making. These aren't topics where you just sit and listen. No, you get involved, laughing and talking with each other, a perfect way to teach sustainability.

A Dark Cloud

We teach children how to measure, how to weigh. We fail to teach them how to revere, how to sense wonder and awe. The sense of the sublime, the sign of the inward greatness of the human soul, and something which is potentially given to all men, is now a rare gift.

— Abraham Joshua Heschel

We must rapidly begin the shift from a "thing-oriented" society to a "person-oriented" society. When machines and computers, profit motives and property rights are considered more important than people, the giant triplets of racism, materialism, and militarism are incapable of being conquered.

— Dr. Martin Luther King Jr.

A dark cloud hangs over this joy and merriment, though. It's been hovering over me as I work on this book. We can't escape it for long. It's our failure to reject the idea that money is the point of life. As Michael Sandel says in *What Money Can't Buy* (2012), markets run our lives. He calls it market triumphalism. We see life as "the economy." Sandel, a professor at Harvard, says that the market extends into every corner of our lives, not just goods and services but family life, friendship, sex, health, education, nature, art, citizenship, and sports. He says we must ask where markets belong and where they don't. We must deliberate about what the good life is.

Of course, this worship of money, this "wealth addiction" as writer Philip Slater called it, is what undermines caring for the common good. Sandel's prescription of "deliberation" is what we need — and can create in the form of study circles. For many years, a lot of us have participated in voluntary simplicity circles. In particular, we have looked at the damage our obsession with wealth has caused.

Pursuit of wealth causes wars — corporations want oil and want to sell their war-related products.

It wastes money — money we should be spending on health and schools and the environment goes to corporate tax breaks.

It increases consumption, which damages the environment — corporations spend lavishly on marketing to get people to consume.

It produces crime — the crimes of high finance remain hidden from us.

It produces corruption — think of the cheating and dishonesty of corporations who overpay their top people and underpay the rest of their employees.

It produces violence — people will do anything to gain more wealth.

It destroys our humanity — in the pursuit of wealth we ignore our values, pursuing profit no matter what the effect on people and the planet.

It isolates us — we're cut off from life because we buy ourselves out of a problem.

It creates suspicion — trust is destroyed because we feel that others are out to get us.

It divides society — the rich are worried the poor will steal from them; the poor know the rich are stealing from them.

And of course, to continue the drum beat — the gap

between the rich and the poor undermines a nation. As we've seen throughout this book, the wealth gap undermines health, happiness, and democracy. Ultimately, we must do something about wealth inequality. Without addressing this, there will be no chance of creating a caring, collaborative culture concerned about the common good.

Voluntary Simplicity

How do we create this caring culture? One of the ways we've been trying to work on this is the voluntary simplicity movement. For several years this was a growing movement of its own, but now the idea of living more simply and cutting back on consumerism has spread and is almost mainstream.

Just as women joined together in consciousness-raising groups to create lives of gender equality, many of us join in simplicity circles to support each other in changing our lives. We challenge the belief that being rich will make us happy. We often make drastic changes. Most of us find ways to spend less so we can afford to work less so we can have the opportunity to pursue our calling — enjoy ourselves and make a difference. We come to understand that "less is more."

But in a wider vision, simplicity is a liberation movement, part of the continuum of the liberation movements of the past 50 years — where we have refused to let the *powers that be* destroy our dignity by the trivialization of our experience. We want free time, free media, freedom from manipulation, freedom to be involved in community and creativity.

People want to liberate themselves from overt and covert oppression that keeps us from living fully; we want to liberate ourselves socially, morally, emotionally, intellectually.

Essentially, voluntary simplicity is "the examined life" — asking what's important and evaluating our behaviors in terms of the well-being of people and the planet. The subtitle of my book *Circle of Simplicity* is *Return to the Good Life*. And that's what we figure out in the study circles — what the good life is. It's about slowing down and savoring life. It's about taking time to appreciate what's around you, finding connection with nature. Breaking free of the corporate, competitive consumer society is tremendously liberating, and it leads to a life of symbolically, if not literally, "dancing in the streets" — entering joyfully into the life of the commons.

Chapter 12

The Remaking of a Counterculture: The Barefoot Teacher

I have no teaching, but I carry on a conversation.

— Martin Buber

All real life is meeting.

— Martin Buber

One day, several years ago, I read a quote from Thoreau, and his words stopped me cold: "We are all schoolmasters and the universe is our school house." When I read that, I felt a shift inside me. I felt that here was another part of the answer I'd been searching for. I, who have been a teacher all my life, suddenly realized that I had missed the real point of my vocation. I had failed to realize that, as Thoreau says, this is *everyone's* true nature — being a teacher. I don't mean the teacher who stands up in front of a classroom and gives lectures and tests and grades. I mean someone who nurtures and inspires and encourages and guides and challenges and supports others by talking with them. At heart, we're all teachers.

At the core of our essential self is the vision of helping others in their search for fulfillment. Think how moved you are when someone asks for advice, and how deeply stirring it is to help open up new possibilities for another person. The essence of each one of us is this impulse to nurture and transform. It's at the center of our true selves, but it's something we have forgotten, that's been buried.

When I saw Thoreau's words, I felt as though they were glowing, calling out to me from the page. But then I thought of some of the teachers I had known. The ones who had bored me, who had humiliated me, who had failed to inspire me. Then I had another one of those flashes of insight. We don't need more classroom teachers, we need *barefoot* teachers. The term *barefoot* didn't just come to me out of the blue. It was buried in my subconscious, a forgotten memory about a time when China trained thousands of lay people in the basics of medicine and health care, and sent them out to the small towns and villages throughout the country. They were called barefoot doctors, and apparently they transformed Chinese health care.

I was always fascinated with that story. And then, a few years ago I discovered that in some African countries the concept still exists, and further, in India there is a barefoot college — a school that encourages villagers to live in sustainable ways, helping them preserve their ancient customs as well as learn new ones that will help them survive.

So, when that term *barefoot* surfaced from my memory, I suddenly saw thousands of teachers spread out across *our* land (from California to the New York Island), inspiring people to lives of joy and meaning, lives dedicated to creating a caring culture committed to the common good.

How do I envision the barefoot teacher? The image of being barefoot suggests certain attributes. They are teachers who are at the same time sensible and idealistic — their feet on the ground, their heads in the stars (a quote from *Harold and Maude*). Being barefoot, they're obviously not dressed for success, so they're certainly not out for power and prestige. There is the suggestion of the pilgrim or pioneer, seeking some new reality. Barefoot teachers would see themselves as being on a special journey or quest. The barefoot teacher is the common, everyday person who commits himself or herself to nurturing the human spirit and inspiring others to work for the common good. As I thought about this idea, I envisioned people who love life, who love other people. I imagined talking with these teachers, and I knew that I would feel enlivened and enlightened. I would be transformed.

But then my imagination began to falter. How many people do I know who love life, who know how to collaborate and cooperate, who understand what happiness really is? Mostly I hear complaints about frantic lives and the stupidity of the public. What would inspire someone to become a barefoot teacher? Have there been barefoot teachers in the past? I realized that, yes, of course there have been. Most of us would list Socrates, Buddha, Jesus, Gandhi, Martin Luther King Jr. — all who transformed people through the power of their words.

These were not common, ordinary individuals by any means, but it occurred to me that I might discover in them the elements that make up a barefoot teacher. What struck me most, as I thought about these leaders, is that they were devoted to engaging others' hearts and minds. They worked to give people a more expansive sense of life. All of them were iconoclasts — questioning and challenging authority and the dominant culture. And they did it all with conversation.

And as I began to think about these teachers, I realized the true role that conversation had played in history. Conversation was so threatening to the status quo that Socrates was killed for asking questions. Jesus was crucified for telling stories. Madame de Stael was banished for holding salons. The tool that barefoot teachers have used throughout the ages is conversation. None of these people were warriors or kings who — we are taught — were the ones who changed the world. They were common, ordinary souls who believed in the power of talking with others. If we can begin to see ourselves in this tradition, our daily conversation will take on new significance. We may not be a Socrates, Buddha, Jesus, or Gandhi, but we can draw on their inspiration to transform our daily exchanges with people.

A Transformed Vision of the Common Good

What was their vision? It's expressed in a document that is relatively recent — the Universal Declaration of Human

Rights, which was developed by the United Nations in 1948 as a response to WWII. When I recalled that this was the document first used in the Highlander Folk School to teach poor Black people to read and write so that they could vote, I went back and reread it. I realized that each time I have read it over the years, I'm blown away. It not only talks about the rights we take for granted — free speech, freedom of religion, freedom of the press, the right of assembly — it goes even further.

It describes human beings as having inherent worth and dignity, born free and equal. It asserts that we should have freedom from fear and want; that everyone has a right to work, to rest, and have leisure; we have a right to an adequate standard of living including food, clothing, housing, medical care, and security in the event of unemployment, sickness, disability, old age or other "lack of livelihood in circumstances beyond control." We have a right to education that shall be directed to the full development of the human personality and to the strengthening of respect for human rights and fundamental freedoms.

These are rights. Food stamps or government assistance is not a handout. It's something we deserve because we're human beings. And we have a right to be free of fear and want. Have you ever thought of that as a right? Human rights are part of the commons. They are things that belong to all of us.

But the declaration doesn't just talk about rights. It says that the government should be the will of the people and that we should act *in a spirit of brotherhood*. (It actually says this.) And this is the clause that floored me: *"Everyone has duties to the community in which alone the free and full development of his personality is possible."* Community is legitimized and affirmed.

My goodness! Why even write this book? It's all there in that document. I don't know about you, but there was not one classroom, either in school or college, in which I studied this document. I must develop a study circle on this. Unfortunately, I don't know how many people would come. Perhaps we can sneak it in at the end of the happiness circle. It certainly flows naturally from the idea of Gross National Happiness. In fact, this is your first real challenge. *You* develop a study circle on this. Just use the method I outlined: a small group of people talking about three questions, the first being about personal experience, the second about cultural forces that defeat your goals, and the third about actions you can take to accomplish your goals.

And let me know what you've done.

A Transformed Vision of Learning

We are also talking about a whole new way to think of learning. Certainly, if we are all teachers at heart, we are also learners. Learning is about the full flowering of the individual, about transcendence — always going beyond oneself, transcending one's limitations. But modern education doesn't have such a transforming vision. It sees us as economic machines, not as glorious expressions of life. Teachers are pressured to prepare students for tests, not to help them develop their full capacities. For the barefoot teacher, every encounter with another person is significant — no one can be pressured or manipulated or ignored. Probably one of the best expressions of this occurred in the life of Jewish theologian Martin Buber, author of *I and Thou*. He told the story of a young man coming to visit him to talk about some important decisions. But Buber failed to really listen, to fully pay attention to him. Later Buber learned that the young man had committed suicide. Buber always felt that if he had really connected with him, the student would have lived.

And so, Martin Buber was inspired to develop his theory of dialogue — the idea that real learning means being in dialogue with all of life and with each other. To Buber, "All real life is meeting." To him, "Every person born into the world represents something new, something that never existed before, something original and unique." Buber said that we can never see others as a means, only as ends. We can't use people for our own desires, but must engage with them for mutual good. What a shocking idea. We live in a culture in which we are constantly manipulating and being manipulated for things like money, status, prestige, and power — a culture in which there is nothing that money can't buy.

We must learn to think of conversation in the context that we are all teachers and that every conversation is a form of learning and transformation. If we believed that everything we say could eventually spark a revolution or save someone's life, we would approach our conversations differently. We must remember that in this philosophy of learning, truth lies within the individual and emerges in conversation.

The Remaking of a Counterculture

This vision of the barefoot teacher has inspired me for many years. But maybe it's too nebulous. I've been searching for other visions of the barefoot teacher to make it more real. Then I found a book that has helped: *Counterculture Through the Ages* by Ken Goffman. He looks at some of the counterculture advocates throughout history, people like Socrates, Keats and Shelley, Thoreau and Emerson, Allen Ginsberg and John Lennon — some of them the same people I identified as barefoot teachers. He says that there has always been a counterculture resisting the mainstream culture, and he lists the characteristics that they all seem to have held: they were antiauthoritarian, egalitarian, and irreverent; they searched for truth within and challenged convention, hypocrisy, and pomposity — always searching for freedom and joy. I love this list. Isn't this what you want? This to me is the barefoot teacher. And there is one characteristic that encompasses all the others — authenticity. That's what all those traits are about.

Authenticity

> *Every man's foremost task is the actualization of his unique, unprecedented and never-recurring potentialities, and not the repetition of something that another, and be it even the greatest, has already achieved.*
>
> — Martin Buber

Before his death, Rabbi Zusya said "In the coming world,
they will not ask me: 'Why were you not Moses?'
They will ask me: 'Why were you not Zusya?'"

— Martin Buber

We live in an inauthentic society. Nothing, from our food to what we see on TV, is real. And as we live in an increasingly unequal society, we focus on creating an artificial image of success and status. But to be joyful, you have to reject the "manufactured image," drop the false front, reject the counterfeit experiences. Christopher Alexander, author of *The Timeless Way of Building,* says it's about being true to one's own nature. "A man is alive when he is wholehearted, true to himself, true to his inner forces."

As it says in *Teaching as a Subversive Activity,* a '60s book on education, we must teach people the art of crap detecting. So many aspects of our lives are counterfeit — the advertising, the political rhetoric, the personalities we assume for work — that we have lost our ability to discern the true from the false. Without the real, we cannot experience life in depth. When barefoot teachers bring people together, they speak honestly, telling their own stories, comparing their stories and trying to discern the truth. They seek out alternative sources of information and share these with others. They encourage others to speak authentically and truthfully by doing so themselves. They have the courage to say that the emperor has no clothes, giving others the courage to say it themselves. As Thoreau said, "Shams and delusions are esteemed for soundest truths, while reality is fabulous."

Critical Thinking

The problem is the spirit of our age: denial of transcendence,
the vapidity of values, emptiness in the heart, the decreased
sensitivity to the imponderable quality of the spirit.... The
central problem is that we do not know how to think ...
how to resist the deceptions of too many persuaders.

— Abraham Heschel

The barefoot teacher takes the critic out of critical thinking. We need to work with each other to find what is true and real, what will lead to a new culture. In the study circle we tell our stories, take action, and then reflect.

Only if we reflect — think our own thoughts, feel our own emotions, search our own experience for meaning — can we keep from being hypnotized by a culture in which everything is for sale. We spend our days plowing through our lists of things to do, never stopping to ask if we should be doing these things, where they're taking us, whether they're fun or not. We have to reclaim the word *study*. The Latin root of *study* is enthusiasm and zest, yet the word as we usually experience it suggests drudgery and tedium.

What a great thing if we all sat down each evening and studied our day — replayed the things that happened to us, re-experienced our emotions, and asked ourselves what we had learned, asked whether our behavior contributed to or detracted from a sense of joy and meaning.

And then, opened our living rooms and invited others to join with us in a study circle, exploring our challenge of creating a new culture.

Dignity

And as we come together to think, talk, and take action, what should we be studying? We'll study the subjects of human nature, happiness, community, sharing, civility, simplicity, and politics. Even thinking about discussing these subjects is exciting. But recently, I discovered a book that explores a subject that is at the heart of it all.

The name of the book is *Dignity: The Essential Role It Plays in Resolving Conflict* (2011) by Donna Hicks, an associate with the Weatherhead Center for International Affairs, Harvard University. Her thesis is that at the heart of every conflict is the human desire for dignity, the desire to be treated by others as if you have worth and value. When your feeling of dignity is violated, you lash out.

Evolution suggests the reason for this response — to survive. If we sense that someone doesn't value us, it could be a sign that they will attack or destroy us. So we strike before they can get us. Sensing a lack of respect is a feeling that warns of possible danger.

On the other hand, when we feel valued and treated with worth, it's a signal that all is well, and we can connect with those other people. They are not out to harm us. With *respect,* we are flooded with feelings of love, empathy, and compassion and we connect with the other.

We continue this today. The *self-preservation* instinct leads us to alienate others; the *self-extension* instinct to build relationships. Hicks suggests that in our hunter-gatherer stage, connection triumphed over disconnection because there was enough food and water for everyone. And this period accounts for 95 percent of human history.

But when we developed agriculture 10,000 years ago, we felt we no longer had enough, and we began to fight over land and developed a fear-based view of others. To protect ourselves we developed hierarchical institutions, institutions that used humiliation and control as a need for survival.

Hicks goes on to say that during the Renaissance, Europeans challenged this and became conscious of the harmful aspects of "ranking" human worth. We have continued ever since to explore the problem of hierarchy and rank — abolishing slavery, giving people equal rights, guaranteeing protection before the law. Now, if we are to survive, we need to continue this and restore our capacity for connection.

To do this, we need to understand how dignity works: when our dignity is abused, when we are treated as if we have no value or worth, we want to attack (fight) or leave (flight) and end the relationship. We must learn to understand how deep a wound this is — that a violation of our dignity feels like a threat to our survival.

Fight or flight is an instinct. Our challenge is to be able to stop and reflect and rise above instinct by making a *conscious* choice about what we should do. Here is the real meaning of education — helping people learn to expand their conscious choices so that they can live fully, helping them learn to choose a path that is in their best interest, helping them to see that their best interest is connected to the best interest of the whole people: the common good. We have to create an environment that helps people come together and reflect on the idea of dignity — the idea that all people must be treated with value and worth.

This is the role of the barefoot teacher: treating everyone with dignity and creating opportunities for people to experience dignity. This is what we do when we invite people into our living rooms to talk. Maybe it's a happiness circle; maybe it's news night; maybe it's a meeting of the Transition movement. Essentially it's conversation in which people apply the ideas of dignity.

At the heart of this conversation is the acknowledgment that we have *all* had our dignity violated and that we have all violated someone else's dignity, even when we didn't realize it. When you learn this, says Hicks, you experience empathy. (Once again, we return to empathy.) We learn to feel what the other person feels and to care for the common good. She quotes George Eliot, saying, "What are we here for but to make life a little easier for one another?"

Finally, Hicks offers words for the barefoot teacher. Yes, anger and resentment are natural reactions to dignity violations, but anger doesn't work. If we can learn to think in terms of dignity, maybe we can learn to feel empathy. Maybe this will help us as we face an uncivil society.

Here are the essential elements of dignity that Hicks has developed in her work. As you'll see, they're very similar to the elements of good conversation.

Acceptance of identity: Don't judge people — particularly in terms of race, religion, gender, sexual orientation, age. This has certainly been the core of the movements in American history.

Inclusion: Help others feel they belong.

Safety: Help people feel safe in your presence, both physically and psychologically.

Acknowledgment: Give people your full attention by "listening, hearing, validating, and responding" to what they say.

Recognition: Notice what people do and show them you appreciate their contributions.

Fairness: Treat people "justly," which means as equals, as humans deserving care. Support the laws and rules of a fair society, and protest the rules that are not fair.

Benefit of the doubt: Treat people in a way that says that you are assuming that they are trustworthy.

Understanding: Act in a way that communicates that you care what they are thinking, that you respect their ideas and feelings; that you would like to know more by talking with them.

Independence: Encourage people to think for themselves and act in their own best interests.

Accountability: Be responsible for your own behavior. If you have violated someone's dignity, apologize and change your behavior.

Incredible! These are the traits of a good conversation. But that's the way powerful ideas are — they emerge from several sources. When times are bad, the answers keep presenting themselves in many forms and many places.

Celebration as the Last Word

> *Every moment is a new arrival, a new bestowal.*
> *How to welcome the moment? How to respond to the*
> *marvel? The cardinal sin is in our failure not to sense*
> *the grandeur of the moment, the marvel and mystery*
> *of being, the possibility of quiet exaltation.*
> — Abraham Heschel

Theologian Thomas Berry has said that each era has its own Great Work, and that ours is saving the planet. But of course, we can't save the planet unless we save its people as well. All the problems are related, and all spring from an unawareness that we are all one, all part of the web of life. Barefoot teachers are like Johnny Appleseed, planting the seeds that help people see that we are part of a glorious, creative universe, that we are each a unique expression of the life force coursing through the cosmos. And above all, the barefoot teacher is deeply rooted in the joyful community and lives his or her life "dancing in the streets."

Only if we realize this — and act on it — will we be able to create a new culture of collaboration, caring, and concern for the common good.

Index

About the Author

C ECILE ANDREWS is a community educator focusing on voluntary simplicity, "take back your time," the "Sharing Economy," and Pursuit of Happiness Conversation Circles. She is the author of *Slow is Beautiful*, *Circle of Simplicity* and co-author of *Less is More*. She has a doctorate in education from Stanford University. Cecile is very active in the Transition Movement in the US. She and her husband are founders of Seattle's Phinney Ecovillage, a neighborhood-based sustainable community.

If you have enjoyed *Living Room Revolution* you might also enjoy other

BOOKS TO BUILD A NEW SOCIETY

Our books provide positive solutions for people who want to
make a difference. We specialize in:

**Sustainable Living • Green Building • Peak Oil •
Renewable Energy • Environment & Economy Natural
Building & Appropriate Technology Progressive Leadership
• Resistance and Community Educational & Parenting Resources**

New Society Publishers

ENVIRONMENTAL BENEFITS STATEMENT

New Society Publishers has chosen to produce this book on recycled
paper made with **100% post consumer waste,** processed chlorine
free, and old growth free.

For every 5,000 books printed, New Society saves the following
resources:[1]

17	Trees
1,518	Pounds of Solid Waste
1,670	Gallons of Water
2,179	Kilowatt Hours of Electricity
2,759	Pounds of Greenhouse Gases
12	Pounds of HAPs, VOCs, and AOX Combined
4	Cubic Yards of Landfill Space

[1]Environmental benefits are calculated based on research done by the
Environmental Defense Fund and other members of the Paper Task Force who study
the environmental impacts of the paper industry.

For a full list of NSP's titles, please call 1-800-567-6772 *or check out our website* at:

www.newsociety.com

new society
PUBLISHERS